Above Hiroshi Hamaya: The Sun at Niigata, 15 August 1945
Following pages Kikuji Kawada: *The Japanese National Flag*, from *Chizu (The Map)*, 1965;
The Atomic Dome, Hiroshima, from *Chizu (The Map)*, 1965.

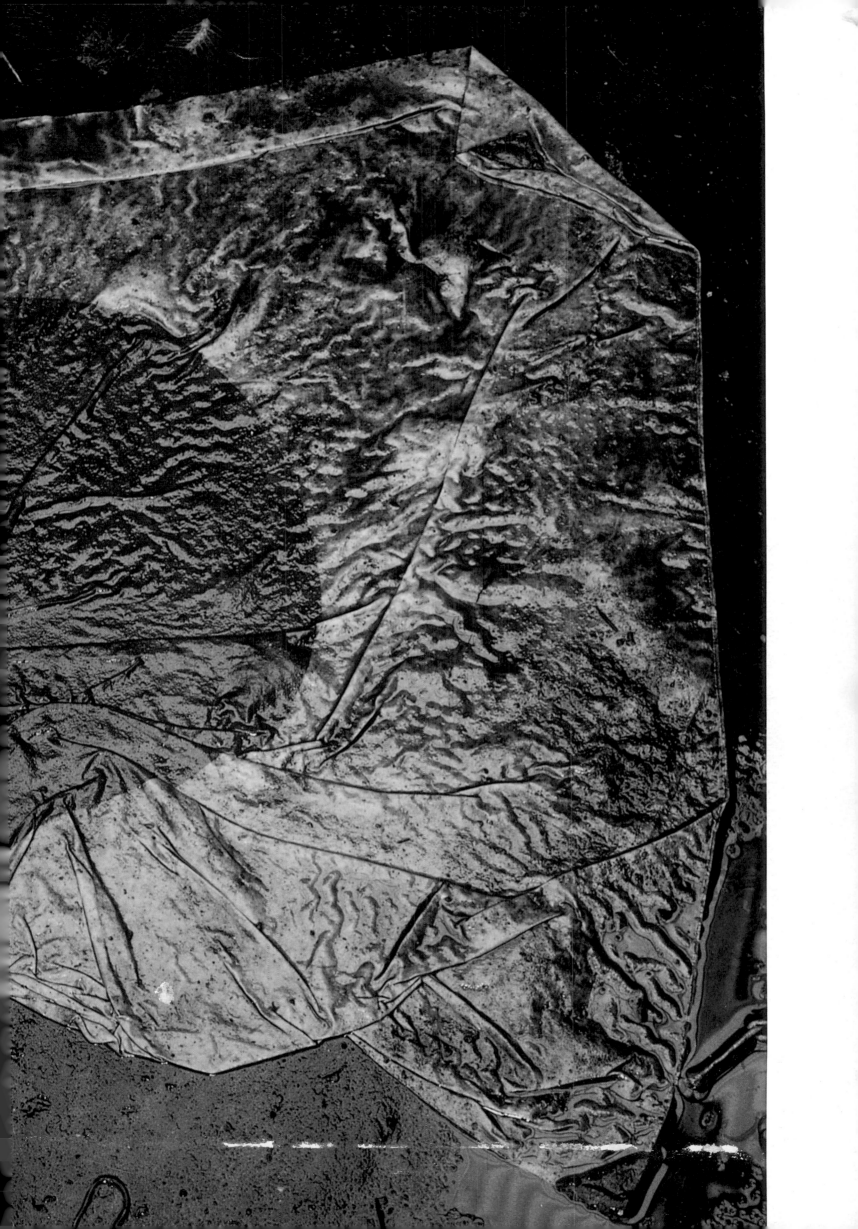

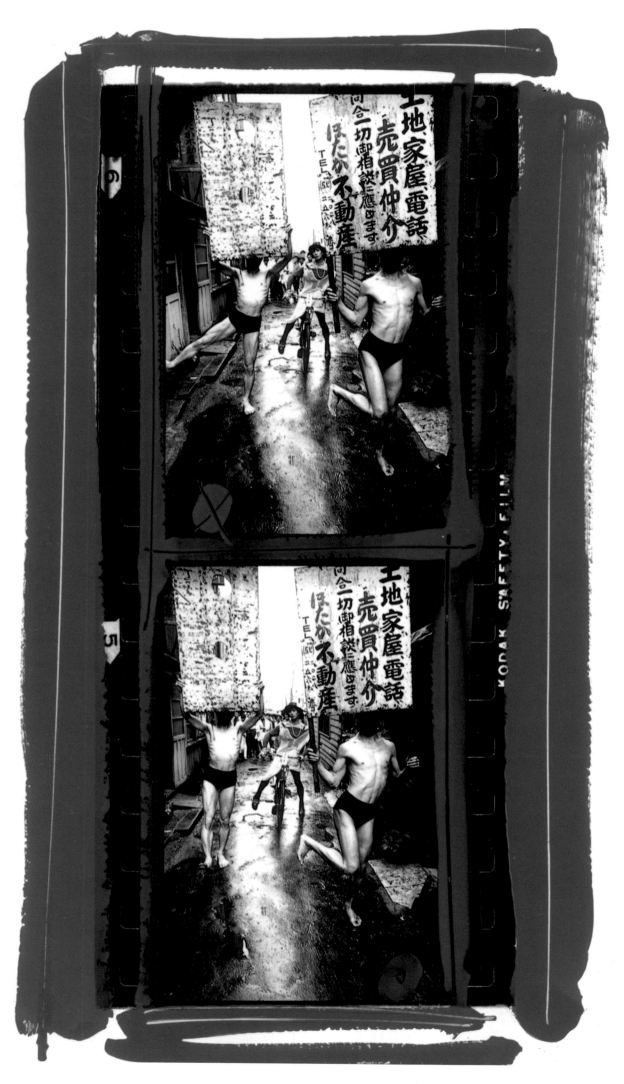

William Klein: *Dancers and Telephone Panels*, Tokyo, 1961

Beyond Japan

A Photo Theatre

Mark Holborn

BARBICAN ART GALLERY
IN ASSOCIATION WITH JONATHAN CAPE
LONDON

FOREWORD

Beyond Japan: A Photo Theatre has been made in recognition of the extraordinary developments at work in Japan since 1945. Over the subsequent forty-five years, the country has experienced a dramatic economic, social and cultural rebirth which has been poignantly witnessed by the photographic process. Indeed, in the exhibition and the accompanying book, the camera appears as a metaphorical part of this rebirth. Since the last world war, the international camera and film industry has become dominated by Japanese products and much of the dynamic, visual artwork made in Japan in the same period has incorporated photography in some measure into its making.

This study, a continuation of Barbican Art Gallery's programme of major photo exhibitions, was commissioned so that it might form a challenging part of the Japan UK Festival in 1991, challenging in the sense of attempting to reveal and/or change British preconceptions about Japanese culture in the forum of a festival that seems to encourage a greater understanding among the British audience about Japan and its people.

Beyond Japan is challenging yet further, in that the study, with its title suggesting a movement *beyond* national boundaries and viewpoints, reflects the country's post-1945 transformation from an introspective cultural entity into an international arbiter of taste, backed by the strength of the country's present financial influence in the world.

It is fitting, therefore, that an exhibition revealing this transformation should be seen in the Barbican Centre, within the City of London, a locality that has such strong business links with Japan, and Barbican Art Gallery is privileged to have received so much enthusiastic support from the exhibiting artists and other colleagues, without whose help this venture would not have been possible. We are also most grateful to QUICK EUROPE LIMITED, a company new to arts sponsorship, for their generous and enlightened support.

John Hoole, Curator, Barbican Art Gallery

DAVID BYRNE

COMME DES GARÇONS

TAMOTSU FUJII

MASAHISA FUKASE

HIROSHI HAMAYA

TATSUMI HIJIKATA

EIKOH HOSOE

EIKO ISHIOKA

KIKUJI KAWADA

WILLIAM KLEIN

SEIJI KURATA

ISSEY MIYAKE

RYUJI MIYAMOTO

DAIDO MORIYAMA

MASATOSHI NAITOH

IRVING PENN

HIROSHI SUGIMOTO

SHUJI TERAYAMA

BILL VIOLA

TADANORI YOKOO

Irving Penn: Issey Miyake design, 1989

CONTENTS

PREFACE

ALMOST TWENTY YEARS ago I arrived in Yokohama on a boat from Siberia. The change in scale was dramatic. Interested in Japanese attitudes to the natural world and in how they influenced architecture and traditional aesthetics, I subsequently wrote a book about Japanese gardens. The day of my arrival in Japan was the first anniversary of the death of the writer Yukio Mishima, whose suicide seemed to elicit an almost embarrassed response among my Japanese friends. A few months later Yasunari Kawabata, Mishima's former teacher, also committed suicide in very different circumstances. Ideas of harmony and space in Japanese design or the aesthetics of the tea ceremony seemed far from the spirit of the nation. As I travelled down the coast of the Inland Sea to Hiroshima, I saw the worst devastation of landscape outside of Vietnam. Photochemical smog was choking the cities. The economic miracle that had been proclaimed was not so simple. I felt a huge sense of crisis.

I stayed for six months and discovered that the Japan of my fantasies did exist, but in remote backwaters and that there was also an astonishing economic momentum, but this was accompanied by profound questions of national identity and direction. I read all translated Japanese literature avidly; Mishima had accused the nation of being drunk with prosperity and I could see some truth in this. At that time victims of mercury poisoning from Minamata were camping outside the headquarters of the Chisso Corporation as part of their battle for compensation. In 1973 a court ruled in favour of the claimants and it was estimated that the terrible poisoning may have affected 10,000 victims. The case demonstrated corporate greed and tragic environmental and human disregard. The *real* Japan was a place where flower arrangement was an art, and the sea was poisoned.

I looked for clear evidence of this crisis and I found it in W. Eugene Smith's great photo-document on Minamata, published in 1975. Among the Japanese photographers I felt I was witnessing the expression of a new visual language. I began to see that photographs evoked memory and the past just as they recorded the present, and when sequenced, photographs formed narrative structures like film. By 1985 I had organised the work I was discovering into an exhibition at the Museum of Modern Art in Oxford and at several American museums with an accompanying book, *Black Sun*. The project drew on the work of four Japanese photographers whom I regarded as pioneers. It told four stories featuring a common, dark thread rooted in the events of 1945. I regarded this as a starting point for a series of projects which might counter our Western fantasies of Japan just as my own preconceptions had been overthrown and continued to be challenged.

By the Eighties I felt that photography itself was in crisis, especially in America where photographic tradition had been usurped by a new generation of artists. In Japan there was an abundance of visual imagery on television, video and posters which was pushing pure photographic art to the peripheries of the culture. I was invited by Barbican Art Gallery to involve the work of fashion designer Issey Miyake and art director Eiko Ishioka in a form of installation that would be theatrical. They represented a culture that emanated from Tokyo but was international: they had both drawn inspiration from Africa and both had lived in the West. They were pioneers who worked beyond a single medium or were in the process of creating their own medium. Their use of photographic imagery was startling, even shocking. Their work suggested a transcultural pattern for the future. They were artists who could take the reader or viewer beyond the clichés of Japan. *Beyond Japan* became the destination of this project, but first I had to create a series of steps that took the reader from the ruptures of 1945, through a Theatre of the Body, a Theatre of Revolt and a Theatre of the Street to a point of future unity which is neither East nor West.

A model for escaping a confined sense of photography was Alfred Stieglitz, who pioneered the art within a wide cultural context in the first decades of the twentieth century. I find Stieglitz constantly inspiring because he crossed boundaries. *Camera Work*, his magazine, contained Gertrude Stein on Picasso; he exhibited African art and children's paintings. He took photography into another dimension and placed it beside the most innovative work. He was laying the creative foundations for his time alongside such giants as Walter Gropius. Beside them, I place the sculptor Isamu Noguchi, who was both Japanese and American. Stieglitz and Noguchi bridged Eastern and Western traditions, not theoretically but expressively. The legacy of their tradition and innovation is passed on to such figures as Issey Miyake or the contemporary Osaka architect Tadao Ando at the end of the century. The recurring motif of this project is a circle.

Beyond Japan is not definitive; it is simply a stepping stone – part of a process. It contains another exhibition which exists only as a fantasy but serves as a ghost to this project, and which includes Alfred Stieglitz, Isamu Noguchi, Issey Miyake and Tadao Ando – a photographer, a sculptor, a fashion designer and an architect. It is through such juxtapositions that I hope to get closer to what I experience, and to move beyond photography as I have attempted to move beyond Japan.

Mark Holborn
London, 1991

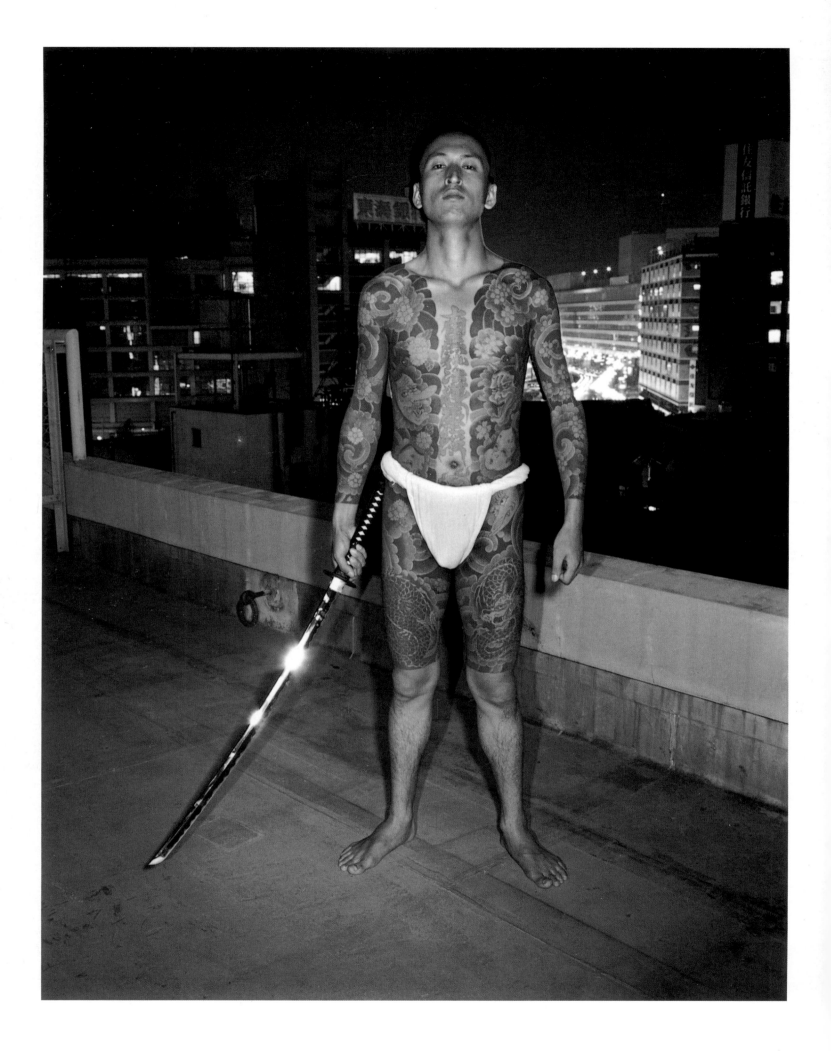

Above Seiji Kurata: Tokyo, 1975, from *Flash Up*, 1980
Following spread Kikuji Kawada: *Map of Japan from the Middle Ages*, from *Chizu (The Map)*, 1965

1

FRAGMENTS ON
THE MAP

JAPAN EXISTS IN my memory as if on a television screen. The camera is moving in close as if descending on the scattered archipelago from space. At first the islands look like an alien planet. Whatever my point of departure, Japan is the opposite pole.

However I reconstruct the images of Japan in my mind, they are bounded by rectilinear form – the frame of cinema, the television screen, the edges of a page, the viewfinder of a camera, or the border of a flag. Our memory of Japan exists as chains of images or mental strips of photographs fed by the graphic nature of its culture. Even Japanese history has been reinvented by cinema and now resides in our imagination in a flow of indelible imagery: choreographed battles, armour pierced by arrows, the *samurai* helmet, the flash of a blade or the border of a *kimono*. These chains constitute the fantasy which we call 'Japan'.

Cartography may be the first form of graphic fiction. Early man looks up at the sun, then down at his feet and inscribes a line through the sand, with which he depicts his place and his route. He invents a line about his destination. For Western man the fiction becomes elaborated through history until he imagines the edge of the world. Eventually after the tales of shipwrecked sailors he knows that somewhere to the eastern edge lies a chain of volcanic islands. This dangerous, exotic place, possibly inhabited by demons, is the antithesis of home. It tempts that part of the imagination that has grown complacent, lazy, or too secure. He is drawn to it because it represents all that he does not know. In the Western tradition of Orientalism it represents the 'other' place.

The recent medium of photography was developed during an age of belief in an absolute world and scientific truth. At the time, it was considered to present an objective view of the exterior world, from the pyramids of Egypt to the face of Alfred Lord Tennyson. The rectangle of photography provided the window on the outside, but its objectivity was as illusory as the moral confidence on which the Victorian empire was

15

founded. When photography reached Japan, it was reinvented by an alien Japanese eye with a graphic virtuosity already evident in *ukiyo-e* prints or *sumi-e* ink painting. Japanese graphic tradition persists from the hieroglyphs of the language to the massive comic industry today, which demonstrates the dominance of the visual image over the word. The photographic image that emerged after World War II formed new sentences in an original, graphic language, which was foreign to our verbal and literate Western culture. Ultimately we are required to redraw our maps and attempt new translations with which to transcend our old fictional 'Japan'.

At the end of World War II, Japan's contact with the modern world had lasted less than a century. Commodore Perry's 'Black Ships' of 1853 had arrived in a world isolated from Western contact, with the exception of the earlier Jesuit missionaries and some stray Portuguese sailors. In the vast, sprawling city of Edo, present-day Tokyo, a collapsing feudal structure had been replaced by the power of a merchant class. After the restoration of the Emperor Meiji (1867–8) and an industrial revolution Japan became the dominant economic force in South-East Asia. With a lack of the necessary raw materials to sustain the revolution, the Japanese began to expand, in accurate emulation of European colonialism.

In nineteenth century Europe the fantasy of Japan had been stirred by artists attracted to the audacious line and colour of the floating world of *ukiyo-e*, and by writers who had conjured up exotic Oriental women. At the same time, the real Japan was set on a determined course that would eventually overwhelm a European power. In an astonishing period Manet had painted Emile Zola in front of his Japanese prints (1868), Van Gogh had also discovered *ukiyo-e* (1886) and Pierre Loti had published *Madame Chrysanthème* (1888). In 1904, the same year as Puccini's *Madame Butterfly* was first performed at La Scala, the Russian army surrendered to the Japanese after a three-month siege at Port Arthur. The following year, the Japanese sunk the Russian Baltic fleet at Tsushima. The twentieth century began with the collapse of an anachronistic Tsarist state and with the ascendancy of an expansionist, modern state, still rooted in divine leadership and mythical imagery. The twentieth century opened with the momentum of a seemingly contradictory Japan.

The dialogue between Japan and the West is frequently described in terms of Japan's absorption of the West. The pattern of imitation, absorption, and finally reinterpretation of Western ideas is explicit, as it was in the Japanese importation of Chinese culture a thousand years before. In contrast, the West's absorption of Japan is inconclusive and rarely described. *Japonisme* was the first stage in the imitation of a Japanese aesthetic. It was primarily decorative and involved the borrowing of Japanese motifs and design elements. Oriental views provided the West with spectacle but the true exchange did not occur until the later recognition of deeper, common sensibilities by writers and artists on opposite sides of the East/West divide.

In 1923, Ananda K. Coomaraswammy, the distinguished curator of Oriental art at the Boston Museum of Fine Art, urged Alfred Stieglitz to make some of his photographs available for the museum, thereby taking the first curatorial stance of recognition. It was the first occasion on which photographs were to be exhibited in their own right on the walls of a museum, not as illustration. Stieglitz had sought to destroy a pictorialist genre of photography and to offer the possibility of an expressive medium that did not borrow from painting. He revealed that the power of a photograph was far greater than the power of the simple, graphic elements of its surface. Stieglitz's photographs were not illustrations of an exterior world, but equivalent to the state of an interior world. He created a language, technically available through the new medium of photography, which could reach areas of experience encountered in great music and art, especially in the meditative qualities of certain Oriental art. Stieglitz emphasised his American identity, yet touched on a universal art.

Stieglitz's photographs showed a pronounced reduction, a stripping away of superfluous elements, a movement towards the uncluttered essence of the image. A branch of a tree just crosses the edge of an almost empty Stieglitz photograph in which clouds swirl or rage. Vast space emanates from even his smallest frames. He could suggest forces as colossal as the ambition in the construction of Manhattan. The sense of scale was quite distinct from the dimensions of his prints. This illusion of space and art of reduction was also evident in Sung Chinese painting and subsequent Japanese painting, where vision of great scope was executed with the simplest brushstrokes.

In 1913 the work of the Romanian sculptor from Paris, Constantin Brancusi, was exhibited at the great Armory Show in New York. It was an occasion championed by Stieglitz as the introduction of the most innovative European art to America. The following year, Brancusi's sculpture was exhibited at Stieglitz's own gallery, 291; it involved a reduction to pure, elemental, even mythical form. In 1927, the young Japanese sculptor Isamu Noguchi, went to Paris to work as Brancusi's assistant. He wrote, 'Brancusi, like the Japanese, would take the quintessence of nature and distil it. Brancusi showed me the truth of materials and taught me never to decorate or paste unnatural materials onto my sculptures, to keep them undecorated like the Japanese house.'*

Noguchi was to spend his life between Japan and America. In 1984, not long before he died, I saw him erecting his monument of a lightning flash pivoting on a point, close to Benjamin Franklin Bridge in Philadelphia. It is a tall, metallic tower which he had designed almost fifty years before. He gleefully watched it as it was positioned. The operation was conducted under the guidance of rocket engineers from NASA. It seemed to be the symbolic fulfilment of aspiration and invention, the qualities of a pioneer. His new museum in Long Island City, New York, exemplifies the elemental purity of Japanese aesthetics. The raw materials of the building and garden are not exotic, imported Japanese rocks and timber, but common American materials. It is the focused simplicity with which they are applied that owes much to a Japanese sensibility, like that of Brancusi. Noguchi is the forerunner of a new generation of artists who have bridged the East/West divide and can no longer suffer the convenience of the label 'Japanese', with all the exotic or alien qualities the label implies. This cross-over has nothing to do with the internationalism of museum or gallery culture, but with the roots of their creativity.

The simplicity of Japanese architecture, especially of such masterpieces as the seventeenth-century Katsura Palace, was an influential model for such pioneers of Western

*Sam Hunter, *Isamu Noguchi*, Abbeville, New York, 1978.

19

modernism as Gropius or Frank Lloyd Wright. Katsura was innovative, yet clearly demonstrated elements of Japanese tradition. Katsura draws the eye into details, into the joinery of the timber, the moss around the stepping stones, the geometrical pattern of a sliding screen, the metal cover over the head of a nail, or the recessed handle on a sliding door. The design allows the eye to focus; it allows the true qualities of the materials to become explicit. The eye returns to the grain of wood or the surface of rock. It is as quintessential as Noguchi suggested of Brancusi. It pervades Japanese design or action from architecture to the tea ceremony. This process of reduction is the opposite of a Western process of construction and elaboration of an image. It is through this tradition that a single brushstroke can suggest a panoramic view of the infinite. The purity of modernism was the key to the ideals of universal modern design. The Bauhaus was a laboratory of reduction, where the cluttered decoration of the nineteenth century was stripped away. Audacious, simple strokes were necessary for a language that could suggest the dynamic of the twentieth century.

Stieglitz, Brancusi, Noguchi, Gropius stand out as established members of a modern, creative pantheon, who were building twentieth-century foundations. They were also figures who, conspicuously or not, worked on a line between East and West. Their lineage should make it possible now to travel outside the fiction of the East, the fantasy of 'Japan'. One must encounter Japan, before one can go beyond it. Visual harmony, exemplified at Katsura, is an invisible characteristic in the blazing, nocturnal cities of Japan. It exists in interior worlds, behind closed doors, or deep within the imagination. A camera eye cannot easily reach such a place; it must first engage with the antithesis of harmony – a landscape of chaos. The lessons of Japan are about responses to the immediate environment, the grain of the wood on which you stand. If we circumscribe a line around the world, we can pass beyond Japan and return to our own hemisphere.

The maps of Japan as late as the Edo or Meiji periods, from the early seventeenth to the early twentieth century, suggest a paradise of mountains, rivers, and small fishing villages, joined by old highways along the coast. Even the city of Edo is illustrated in the maps of the time as a city of logical harmony with a grid system. The new city that has grown from the postwar rubble still hides its secret quarters, the vestiges of the narrow lanes of Edo culture, or the old Tokyo of Ozu's films. Street vendors, gangsters, and bar girls inhabit an underworld far below the surface of the city, down alleys too small to be marked on any map.

The large, green space at the centre of any map of Tokyo marks the grounds of the Imperial Palace, an axis of the nation like Mount Fuji itself. In an environment where space is the most valuable commodity, the significance of this patch of green could be judged by its sheer size. The other green zones mark territories for historical ghosts such as the Emperor Meiji or the Yasukuni shrine for the war dead. These scattered points of memory are constants, as fixed as the *torii* archways of their entrances, against the transitory city that surrounds them. The city radiates out into a maze traversed by railway track and expressways, looping in and out and over each other. Trains pass through the middle of buildings several storeys above the ground. The aerial photographs of the city seem impenetrable as the camera descends. Tokyo seems unchartable.

Driving from the airport to the centre of the city, I look out as though seeing Japan for the first time. The fields below, the bamboo on the hillside, the heavy, sloping curves of a country shrine were there centuries before the landscape depicted by the *ukiyo-e* masters, Hokusai or Hiroshige. The bulldozers have ravaged the hills with savage cuts. Concrete, not timber, is the ubiquitous material. Grey is the first colour in the new spectrum. In winter, the paper-brown rice fields meet the brown bamboo and the dark brown soil beneath the bulldozers, which meets the grey of the open quarries. I see dead trees on the skyline, jets overhead, and security police in riot gear at the toll barriers. Next, the signs of power are visible: railway tracks, electricity generators, orange pylons, cables criss-crossing the land. Where the fields end, enormous, balconied slabs of housing rise from the plain. Their inhabitants dwell in a wilderness. At night they can watch the lights of the streaming traffic from their windows. In such a place, the inner world of the television screen is a means of survival.

Closer to the city the spectrum shifts, signs are written: black characters on yellow background, electric-blue neon, blue-tiled roofs, aerials across the skyline. I pass streams and canals, boats at their moorings, logs on the water, ships moving out to Tokyo Bay. Before I cross the Edo river, Disneyland sprawls on the plain with the spires of a cinematic castle. I am approaching a city that has been pre-empted by cinema. To my foreign eye, the city itself has the quality of a film location. The towers of Shinjuku are glimpsed, rising as a backdrop on a futurist set.

One morning in early summer 1989, on just such a journey, I was thinking about the possible shape of the city over the next decade. I reached the middle of the city and passed the Imperial Palace. There was a crowd at one of the entrances, where cars were parked beside lights and television crews. The Emperor was dying. I was arriving at the moment the key participant in modern Japanese history, a once-divine figurehead, was departing. The leader, who had announced the unthinkable surrender in the face of an unthinkable weapon in 1945, would be dead as the twentieth century, which had opened with the rise of Japan, was drawing to a close. The Showa Era was ending. The moment was a significant juncture, balanced between historical memory and futurist aspiration.

The Emperor had lived through an inevitable rearrangement of the hierarchy of national values following the traumatic events of 1945. The Japanese people had experienced unprecedented loss and destruction. They were obliged to accept the removal of Imperial divinity, the dismantling of national institutions such as State Shinto, and the arrival of a foreign army of occupation. The immediate postwar primary emphasis would have been on food, clothing and housing. The substance of survival would have replaced the rhetoric of war and sacrifice.

There are many photographs of the destruction; the aftermath of the firebombing of Japanese cities was well documented. There is even a handful of photographs of Hiroshima taken only hours after the explosion, but just as the implications of the event were unknown, so it was impossible for the camera to record the full significance. It would take years for any meaning to be decipherable. The event was almost indescribable. Robert Oppenheimer had referred to 'the sun brighter than a thousand suns', from the Bhagavad Gita, when he

Kikuji Kawada: *Photograph and Personal Effects, Special Attack Corps,* from *Chizu (The Map),* 1965

witnessed the atomic tests at Los Alamos. The only image that could accommodate the event was mythical and solar.

The year 1945 is point zero from which all we understand of contemporary Japan must be measured. The foundations of Japan, from the divinity of the Emperor to the basis of the Shinto religion, were destroyed in the few seconds of the nuclear explosions and the subsequent surrender. The first technique in the face of catastrophe is one of mechanical objectivity, through which extreme and volatile emotions are held in check, in the manner in which one might clear the human debris of disaster. This objectivity might allow scientists to measure levels of radioactivity at the site of a nuclear tragedy, because their task would be singular and focused. For the writer it is more difficult to reach an objective tone. John Hersey constructed his famous account of Hiroshima out of an accumulation of eye-witness descriptions as if he was gathering the fragments of evidence, however harrowing their substance.

Czeslaw Milosz stated in *Ruins and Poetry* that 'man constructs poetry out of the remnants found in ruins', when comparing the disintegration of Poland during the years of World War II with that of language itself. As the nation was shattered, poetry became fragmented and stripped of metaphor. The experience of the Warsaw uprising of 1944 and the subsequent destruction of the city was described many years later by a witness through condensed moments or a string of details. 'Human affairs are uncertain and unspeakably painful, but objects represent a stable reality, do not alter with reflexes of fear, love or hate and always behave "logically",' wrote Milosz.

An objective strategy was the inevitable course for a Japanese photographer in the aftermath of 1945. The nation had been moving towards mass sacrifice as if in a trance. After two flashes of destruction the trance was over and the Emperor had uttered the unthinkable. General MacArthur had arrived on Japanese soil wearing sunglasses and black men driving jeeps were cruising what was left of the Ginza. To record this boundless loss and the extent of the rubble was impossible. Ken Domon of the Shudan Group who practised an objective documentary style, began his heroic record of Hiroshima. Thirteen years after the war, his book was published. It addressed the world with a jacket designed from a painting by Joan Miró. Domon's photographs were reproduced in gravure, as if they were illustrations of precious artefacts. He moved his camera close into surgery and scar tissue. He photographed the subject of pain as if the flesh was as inanimate as classical sculpture – an accumulation of gestures, of wrists, hands and masks. The language was monumental.

There is a story of a house-painter at Hiroshima who was close to the epicentre of the explosion. He was up a ladder at the time. His shadow was permanently etched by the blast. There are photographs of such shadows at several places in the city as if the event had transmuted living bodies into invisibility leaving only ghosts. These monuments to humanity were marked for history by the very absence of the physical. Shadows on stone and brick constituted the remnants or fragments of people.

The explosions involve a rearrangement of time. At the actual atomic moment, time is suspended. Time before and time after the event are different; history has changed for everyone. Despite the scale of the events historically, scientifically and philosophically, the

Following spreads Kikuji Kawada: *The Ruin of a Stronghold; Ceiling of Atomic Dome,* Hiroshima; *Scribbling by Tourists, Atomic Dome.* All from *Chizu (The Map),* 1965.

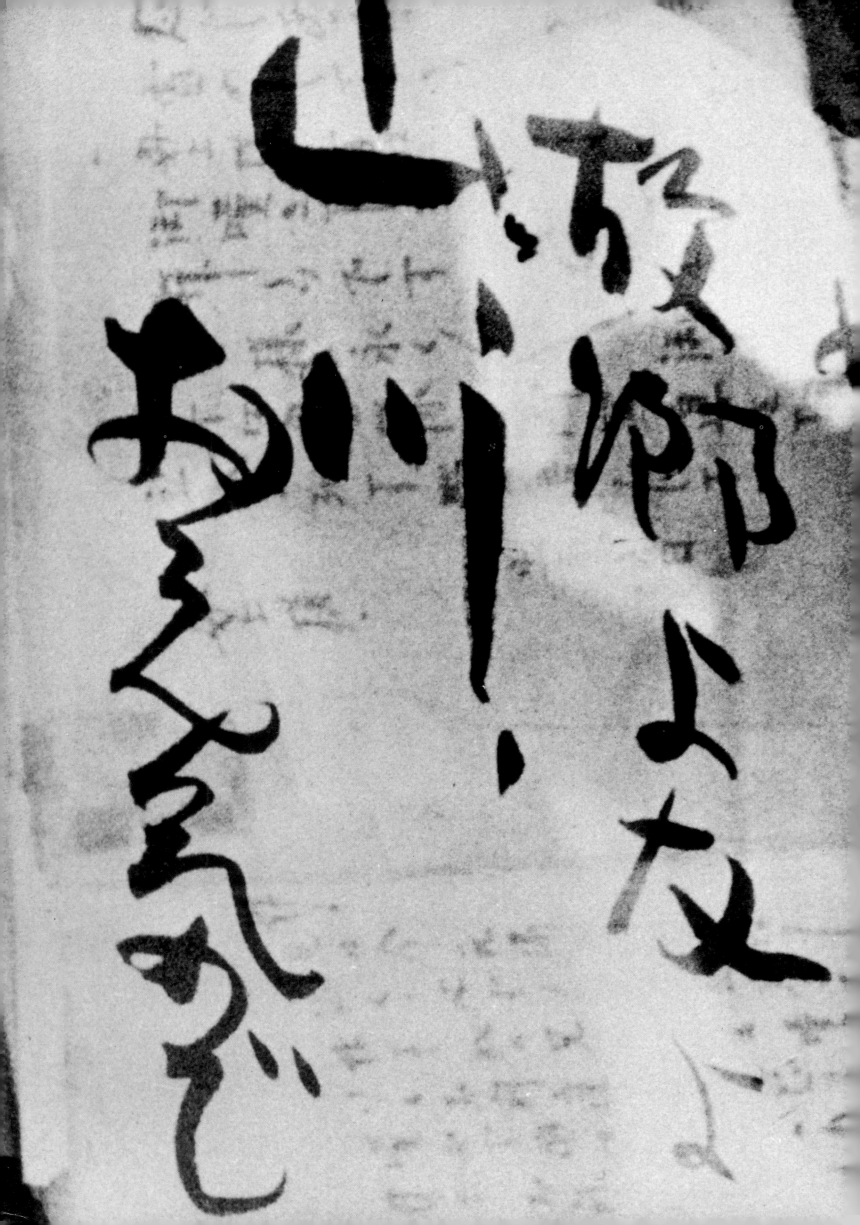

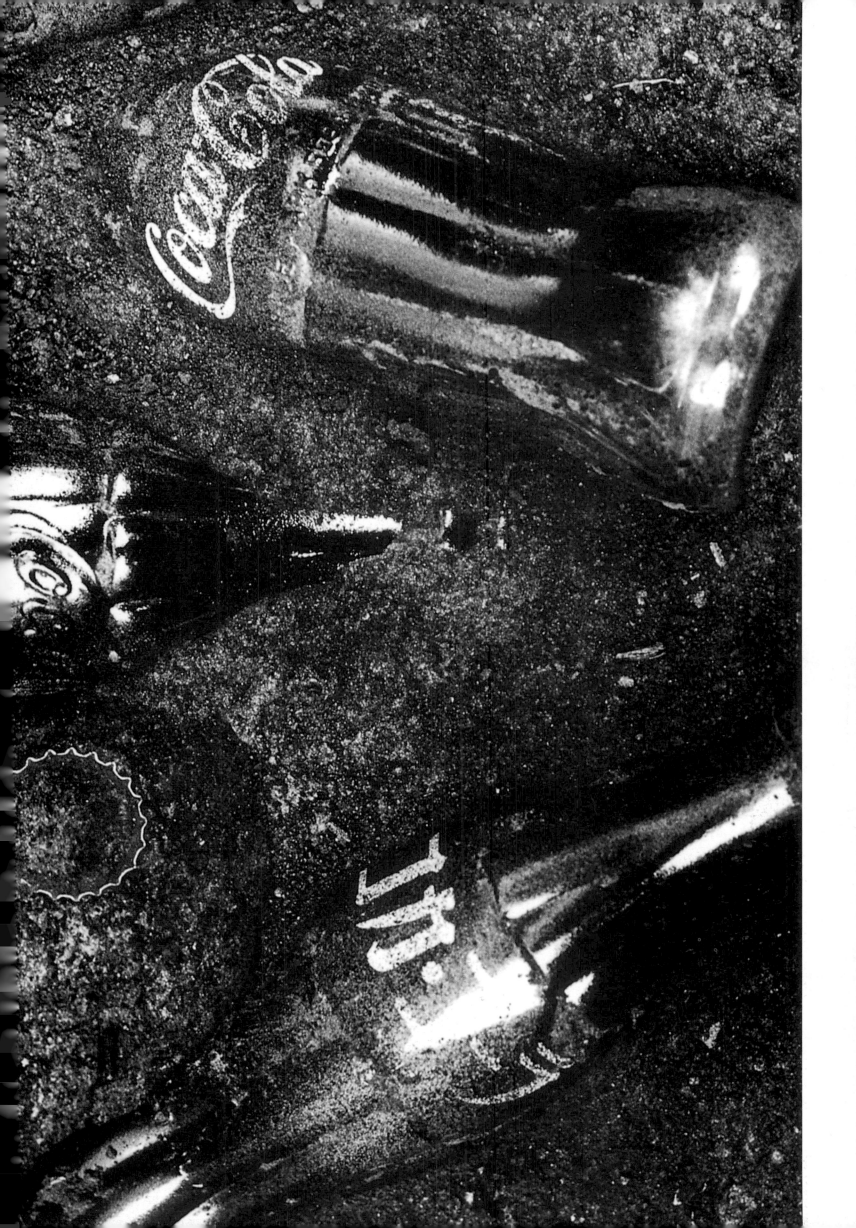

language of atomic weaponry has indeed been neutralised, then mistranslated. In Shibuya, at the centre of Tokyo, close to the densest intersection in the world, where thousands of Japanese youth travel each day to shop, there is now a shoe store called A-Bomb. In fact, it is a remarkably conservative shop. In a single generation the event has been assimilated and resurfaces inconspicuously in the sign language of the city, still further emphasising the inadequacy of the word to describe the event. The most profound events in Japanese history resurface in the most mundane context in the heart of Tokyo, while in the West we are still grappling with the implications of those events.

There is a photograph by Shomei Tomatsu of a watch from Nagasaki, with its hands stopped precisely at two minutes past eleven, the time of the explosion. The circular watch face in the square frame of the photograph was the cover image of Tomatsu's first book *11.02: Nagasaki* (1961). Tomatsu was heralded as a pioneer, the first of a new generation of post-war photographers who were looking for their roots in the aftermath of the Occupation. His subjects were explicitly clear. He engaged in a long-term commitment to photographing around the American bases in Japan and Okinawa, and he travelled to Nagasaki. His Nagasaki book opens with a sequence of fragments: the watch, a scorched sake bottle, burned bamboo, a melted beer bottle glowing like meat on the butcher's hook, a severed finger, a rosary and a decapitated statue. In a few pages, Tomatsu encompassed the scale of the event in both immediate human terms and in a historical perspective, not by what the camera defined but by what the camera suggested; yet the evidence was as clear and factual as any 'objective' document. He wrote, 'We must try not to neglect resisting the natural erosion to which memory is subject. We must build a dam against the flow of time with our will and pull back the time during which memory weakened.'

With the economic recovery firmly established in the Sixties, culminating in the Osaka Expo of 1970, memory of events as terminal as those of 1945 was counter to the momentum of the age. Vast industrial expansion was coupled with a rise in consumerism. A collision between national optimism and the memory of collective loss could provide a profound crisis. A generation had lost not only their families in the war, but also their own childhood. They had become adults in a devastated world under Occupation. With economic recovery in the Sixties came the inevitable shift in the hierarchy of values, from the drive to satisfy physical necessity to questions about national destiny and identity. At a moment of great economic drive in the external world, it was predictable that some internal exploration would take place as if to recover a lost adolescence or to reinvest in memory. There was the need to halt the erosion that Tomatsu described and also to redraw the map and assert a sense of personal place and history at a time when the nation was being so radically transformed. It had taken nearly two decades to find a visual language sufficient to describe the immensity of events. Photography grew not as a method of recording the present through the objective window on the world, but as a medium for evoking the past.

This archaeology, this digging for artefacts or shards of history with which to chart identity, was defined by Kikuji Kawada in his work *Chizu* (*The Map*, 1965). It is a small, black book containing many pages that fold out expansively with an illusion of great scale. Its darkness, with the blackest gravure printing, enables the lines or points of light to acquire an intensified whiteness, through which is conveyed the glare of radiation.

Previous spreads Kikuji Kawada: *A Note Left Behind by Special Attack Corps*; *Coca-Cola*; *Lucky Strike*.
All from *Chizu (The Map)*, 1965.

A photograph of the ruined dome at Hiroshima forms a circle at the opening to the book as the camera points up through the shell of the building to the clouds above. The circular pattern is repeated in the crumpled Japanese flag with its network of lines, or in a discarded pack of Lucky Strike cigarettes. The evidence of Occupation continues in discarded Coca-Cola bottles. These fragments alternate with pages of pure, abstract surfaces, mottled and corroded. They are photographs from the scorched walls of Hiroshima. The crevices in the concrete appear to be melting, running in black, as if the walls were bleeding. Kawada photographed the lines of graffiti gouged into the walls of the gun fortifications around Tokyo Bay. His ruptured world extends to pictures of the last remnants of the kamikaze, the Divine Wind; at the museum of Etajima he photographed their letters, final poems and torn uniforms.

In an introduction to *Chizu*, the writer Kenzaburo Oë referred to the violent light of the work. Yukio Mishima later referred to the same light in his essay *Sun and Steel* (1970), when he described his encounter with the Sun.

> My first – unconscious – encounter was in the summer of the defeat, in the year 1945. A relentless sun blazed down on the lush grass of that summer that lay on a borderline between the war and the post-war period – a borderline, in fact, that was nothing more than a line of barbed wire entanglements, half broken down, half buried in summer weeds, tilting in all directions . . .
>
> That same sun, as the days turned to months and the months to years, had become associated with a pervasive corruption and destruction. In part, it was the way it gleamed so encouragingly on the wings of planes leaving on missions, on forests of bayonets, on the badges of military caps, on the embroidery of military banners.

Kawada was making a similar set of poetic equations in the midst of the relics: the iris of an eye in a shattered dome, the crumpled sun in the flag, the insignia, the memory of the chrysanthemum, the Imperial crest, dead kamikaze pilots, an ancient map, the concrete of abandoned defences and black walls bleached by this violent light.

There are parallels in this language to the work of Anselm Kiefer, the great painter of rust, decay, and war-torn landscape. Kiefer was born in the year 1945 in the Donaueschingen region of Germany. Like his colleagues Georg Baselitz and Marcus Lüpertz, Kiefer feared a loss of German identity. In addition to growing up in an Americanised post-war Germany, he was also resisting the overwhelming influence of American art. He embraced Germanic myth. His range of colours shifted from greys to browns to black, a spectrum of decay in a gloomy, ravaged Europe. By applying straw to the canvas, his paintings acquired the substance of fragments. Kiefer's vision, which follows Kawada's work by twenty years, in another defeated nation, on the other side of the world, shares a common loss and a common form. In *Eisen-Steig (Iron Path,* 1986), grey railway tracks lead to the horizon in a literally terminal vision. Kiefer's sculpture *Zweistromland (The Land of Two Rivers or The High Priestess,* 1985–1989), consisting of two steel bookcases and two hundred enormous lead books, is a profound culmination of his work. The lead pages contain photographs of clouds, images of nuclear rods, rubble, human hair and corroded surfaces. The bookcases are labelled Tigris and Euphrates after the sources of Western civilisation. In addition to the irony of the sheer weight of lead pages, the lead is the symbolic shield. The books form an arcane post-nuclear library.

In his introduction to Kiefer's work, Dr Armin Zweite quotes from Leonardo da Vinci's treatise on painting. 'If you look at a plaster wall with many marks on it, or a stone wall made up of differently coloured stones, you will discover similarity with landscapes and the mountains, shores, rocks, trees, plains, green valleys and hills of every kind.'

These corroded surfaces, like the crumpled Japanese flag, constitute the map itself. They form landscapes in which similar discoveries of loss or displacement can be found, whether it be in Germany or Japan, East or West.

In the summer of 1989 I was walking on a black, volcanic beach in Chiba Prefecture, with Shomei Tomatsu. He had been recovering from an illness and had been photographing a world that was closest to him. The beach was his inevitable subject. Even there he found a terminal landscape; plastic, pounded by the waves and swept in on the surf; dead seabirds scattered among the plastic lines and netting. The waste of Japan's economic transformation was his new fragmentary subject.

There was the sound of a motor and a jeep arrived, sprouting aerials. Across its side was written in large letters JEEP. It carried surfers in lime green and electric pink suits, matching the colours of the plastic that littered the sand. The young driver, cap pulled down low, wearing Ray-Bans, looked like a young General MacArthur. This was the invasion force, the army of Occupation. History itself had turned full circle within the space of a single generation.

Back in Tokyo I found myself staying near Yasukuni Jinja, the shrine to the war dead, which I had visited many times. In the early morning I walked through the great gates to the shrine with their gold imperial crests and to one side I noticed the Yushukan, a wide two-storeyed building which housed the memorabilia of war. It had been closed down in 1945 but reopened in the Eighties. Martial music was playing through loudspeakers as I entered. I wandered around, looking at the armour, swords and arrows, then among the tattered and stained uniforms from the Russo-Japanese War as I passed through the twentieth–century rooms. Manchuria, Pearl Harbor, Saipan, Iwojima followed as place names represented by letters, medals, official portraits, uniforms and paintings, culminating in a human torpedo and a vast panorama of the Divine Thunderbolt Corps attacking Okinawa. The fragments of war were now re-entering public acceptability. Outside the building stood the statue of a divine war-horse, by whose hooves someone had placed a bundle of carrots.

I walked back from the shrine by the green waters of the moat surrounding the Imperial Palace, and passed under an avenue of cherry trees to where I was staying. Waiting for me in my room was a package containing a book entitled *Architectural Apocalypse* (1988) by the photographer, Ryuji Miyamoto, with an essay by the architect, Arata Isozaki. It began, 'The city of the future lies in ruins.' I was leaving the next day and felt impatient and pressured. After reading the first sentence I glanced through Miyamoto's photographs and realised that I had inadvertently found what I had come for. Isozaki, inspired by these photographs, had drawn a circle, so succinctly linking past and future, making sense out of the fragments and creating vision out of the rubble.

Throughout the Eighties Miyamoto had photographed the demolition of buildings from Tokyo to East Berlin, London, Brussels and Vienna. He had also photographed inside the dark, closed world of the walled city of Kowloon. Many of the buildings happened to be cinemas and theatres. They were captioned with the original date of the completion of the building, the name of the architect and the date of Miyamoto's own photograph. The passage of time from creation to destruction is stated.

In 1962 Isozaki created a photomontage he called *Future City* in which new architecture was integrated with historical ruins. He added the caption, 'The Incubator Process. Ruins lie in the future of our city, and the future city itself will lie in ruins.' He was attacking a flawless idealism of the future, prevalent in the architectural aspiration of Japan in the early Sixties, where no vestige of the past or rubble of history remained. It was impossible for Isozaki to conceive of a city that did not accommodate ruins. He remembered the final day of the war, the cloudless, blue sky, the shadows and the brilliant sunlight. 'As my gaze returned to earth, my widened eyes beheld as they could see an almost uniform plane of broken, jagged, charred and burnt-out ruins.' An unblemished, shadowless Utopian future did not correspond to what he or his generation had witnessed.

There is an aesthetic of decay deep in Western romanticism. We all inhabit the fantasies of mythical ruined cities. Isozaki pointed out that Albert Speer believed that the Third Reich should have been designed according to the 'Laws of Ruins'. Miyamoto's ruins, especially those of cinemas and theatres, or most conspicuously those of the Tsukuba Expo site from 1985, where the future of Japanese technology was presented, are relics from lost cities now surpassed not by the ruins of fabric and matter but by the ruins of technology. Ruins so emphatically state the passing of one system or order. It is a point of beginning as well as loss. The fragments that Isozaki finally recognised were technological waste like heaps of electronic circuits, redundant space stations, collapsed robots. The map he recognises is the human brain, marked by the circuitry of the imagination.

Ryuji Miyamoto: *Asakusa Shochiku Movie Theatre*, Tokyo – completed 1929, photographed 1984

Ryuji Miyamoto: *Asakusa Shochiku Movie Theatre*, Tokyo – completed 1929, photographed 1984

Ryuji Miyamoto: *Pavilion Theatre, London*, 1986

Ryuji Miyamoto: *Pavilion of Expo '85*, Tsukuba – completed 1985, photographed 1985

Ryuji Miyamoto: *Pavilion of Expo '85*, Tsukuba – completed 1985, photographed 1985

2

THE THEATRE OF THE BODY

IN CHINESE AND Japanese art there is no history of the nude. Where a human figure occurs within a Sung landscape painting, the figure is an incidental brushstroke, as significant as the line of a tree or a rock. The figure is an intrinsic part of the landscape, not the dominant feature in the foreground. Man and his world are a continuum. The idealisation of the human form is absent, since the figure is no more the active agent than the season or landscape it inhabits.

In Western tradition the primary aspect of Apollo is the embodiment of the solar energy in which the Greeks saw a power that was both creative and destructive. In their rational world he accommodated both light and darkness. He was perfectly balanced and applied his illuminating reason as the god of justice. He suggested a point of equilibrium between black and white. Clarity and balance were represented in perfect proportion in the figure of Apollo. His divine body corresponded to a mathematical aesthetic just as he exercised a purely rational judgment.

The origins of the classical figure lie in this idealised human symmetry. Apollo's form marks the beginning of the theme of the nude, which recurs throughout Western art from the classical world to the twentieth–century innovations of Picasso. Athleticism and mathematics were joined in corporeal harmony as the muscles of the athletes and temple builders were exposed beneath the Mediterranean sun of classical Greece. Leonardo da Vinci placed idealised human proportions at the centre of the Renaissance world of scientific discovery. However, the external, physical form, the world of the flesh, became separate in mortal beings from the world of the spirit. Christian iconography in the *pietà* or the crucifixion represents the body from which the soul has departed. The division of body and soul is fundamental.

Chinese tradition, which was so influential in Japan, assigns the division of spirit and body into the separate realms of heaven and earth. The body is in total correspondence to the universe, 'His round head is the celestial vault, his square feet one with the image of the earth, his hair is the stars . . . his four limbs are the four seasons, his five internal organs, the five elements.'* The interior body, particularly the organs, correspond to elements, colours and cardinal points, as if the microcosm of the interior landscape is aligned with macrocosmic dimensions. From physiology to painting there is a system of integration with profound distinction in perception from that of the West. The Oriental emphasis is holistic and suggests an integrated world like a hall of mirrors, which forms a whole image through an infinitely reflected pattern. The emphasis is on the resolution of duality. Male and female, mountain and valley, heaven and earth, body and spirit and East and West are not divided entities.

Photography reveals that the human body did not conform to the idealisation with which art had elevated it. Photographers began by arranging bodies into positions entirely derivative of the postures of art. There is an abundance of reclining nudes in early photography, which range from the exquisite odalisque to blatant pornography. The imitation may not have been entirely conscious as artistic tradition may have fundamentally rearranged perception of the body. By 1918 Stieglitz's relationship with Georgia O'Keeffe had found expression through revolutionary nudes in which O'Keeffe's body was framed in detail, at close proximity, with great intimacy. Stieglitz's vision was once again established by his art of exclusion, by what he did not allow in the frame. Without debt to iconography or the canon of painterly positions, he allowed the fragments of the flesh to suggest the extent of the whole body. These fragments – hands, breasts, belly – constituted his cumulative portrait, reflecting O'Keeffe's power, sensitivity and sexuality. These photographs correspond to the way Stieglitz saw, not to images of art or to other photography. From the late Twenties and throughout the Thirties, the nude was the common subject of photographic exploration, especially for the inventions of surrealism which required an arena for eroticism.

In 1922 Stieglitz was visited by Edward Weston for the first time. He was shown a number of Weston's prints, including a photograph of a breast from 1920 which he admired. It was a significant moment for Weston as an artist and it filled him with confidence. He began a process of reduction. 'These simplified forms I search for in the nude body are not easy to find, nor read when I do find them,'† he wrote in 1927 when he was searching for pure, simple lines in sections of the body. Weston realised that these sections had a power of connection; they did not occupy disparate existences. He also declared he had 'no suggestion, no allegiance to any other medium'. His art of reduction, like that of Stieglitz, released the great potential of suggestion of the whole. 'I have come to realise life as a coherent whole, and myself as a part, with rocks, trees, bones, cabbages, smokestacks, torsos, all interrelated, interdependent – each a symbol of the whole. And further, details of these parts have their own integrity, and through them the whole is indicated, so that a pebble becomes a mountain, a twig is seen as a tree,' he wrote in California in 1930 as

*From *Huainanzi*, a Taoist encyclopedia from the second century BC, quoted in Jean Levi, 'The Body: The Daoist's Coat of Arms', *Fragments for a History of the Human Body, Part One*, Zone 3, New York, 1989.

†*Edward Weston Nudes*, Aperture, New York, 1977.

if he was on the other side of the Pacific a thousand years before.

This suggestion of totality is clear in the evidence of archaeology as the fragments of classical art were excavated. Magnificent Greek torsos acquire a presence by virtue of their fragmentary nature like the power of an incomplete Cézanne painting or the Leonardo cartoon to which is added the mysterious dimension of unknown possibility. The art of suggestion is more evocative than the statement of definition.

At the time Weston was understanding ideas of coherence and interrelation, Japanese photographers had discovered the nude was a legitimate subject. Throughout the Thirties Japanese architects, graphic designers and photographers had been influenced by modernist, constructivist and surrealist trends from Europe and America. As Japan continued its massive industrial development, modernist design and architecture were absorbed and reinterpreted in a Japanese context. Photomontage and surrealist experimentation were as evident as the lingering pictorialist style of photography that had been derived from Western models, or from the studios of Western photographers in Japan.

The events of World War II then implied an unprecedented violation of the body. The photographs in the Japanese archives of the aftermath of a single fire-bombing raid over the capital are almost inconceivable as evidence. The destruction of Hiroshima was both physical and metaphysical. Death and the splitting of the atom were part of the same equation. After 1945 the balanced symbol of the classical figure of Apollo had been ruptured, along with reason. The weapon of unknown destructive power was rationalised as a saver of life, a peacemaker. After 1945 language could assume open contradiction.

In the mid-Thirties both Stieglitz and Weston had encouraged the artist Frederick Sommer, who was living in Arizona and making photographs. He also had surrealist connections through his friendship with Man Ray and Max Ernst in California. In 1939 Sommer began to photograph the discarded entrails of chickens. In the same year a doctor showed him the amputated foot of the victim of a train accident, which he photographed exquisitely. During the war years the subjects of his photographs included dead coyote, dead rabbits, smashed glass and horizonless images of the Arizona desert. Sommer remained in Arizona, removed and deeply preoccupied with metaphysics and aesthetics. His writing emphasised the links between art and science, aesthetics and technology. He commented that 'The world is not a world of cleavage at all, the world is a world of bonds.' In the climate of mid-century crisis Sommer not only expanded the possibility of what was photographable, but demonstrated that photography could act as a bonding agent, could resolve cleavage, and could create unity out of discarded elements, even out of flesh itself. Sommer made several references to the alchemical tradition, invoking the name of Paracelsus, the sixteenth-century Swiss physician whose life ended in nomadic exile, and with whom Sommer may indeed have identified. Photography was an alchemical process in that it demonstrated the power of transmutation. Detritus, decay and smashed shards, even the emptiness of the Arizona desert, were re-ordered and vitalised by both the chemistry and by the rectangular frame of the photograph. The image was inevitably an extension of an image from the interior world of the photographer, which in turn was derived from a wider world. He re-ordered the ruptures and made patterns, like the chains of poetic language, building the links between the pieces, so reconstituting the body.

In Japan after the war a sense of a new language of the body was created through dance. *Die Neue Tanz* from Germany had been introduced before the war, but it was now accompanied by the first sounds of jazz and flamenco. A theatre of dance could define the body with the stage, as the frame enclosed the photograph. The demarcation of space was fundamental; theatrical space was traditionally defined by a fence of woven bamboo, *takeyarai*, just as sacred space was defined by a fence at the ancient Shinto shrine at Ise. Theatre was an illusory, transient world, as *ukiyo-e* suggests, yet it pervaded all areas of Japanese life as if gesture and action, from the martial arts to the tea ceremony, superseded the abstractions of thought and analysis. Theatrical space concentrated a sense of performance that existed on all levels of daily life. The stage was a place where dualities were resolved, or in the traditional dictum of the painter, where you did not paint bamboo, you became bamboo.

In 1959 a young dancer, Tatsumi Hijikata, staged a famous dance adaptation of Yukio Mishima's novel *Kinchiki* (*Forbidden Colours*, 1951) in a small theatre in Tokyo. The performance reflected the homoerotic themes of the novel and involved the killing of a chicken on stage. Hijikata encountered taboos and created shockwaves. He was subsequently outlawed by the official Japanese dance society. Mishima, who was in the audience, greatly admired Hijikata, whom he regarded as a man of the body, in contrast to his own cerebral preoccupation as a writer. Also present was the photographer, Eikoh Hosoe, who was fascinated by the emergence of new dance and was associated with Akiko Motofuji, a dancer who was to become Hijikata's wife. Hosoe was stunned by Hijikata's performance and went backstage to meet him. Hijikata had demonstrated the first signs of his genius. He was creating his own language, drawing deeply on his childhood and upbringing and delving into the subconscious. At the time of his death in 1986, Hijikata was a revolutionary force in modern dance but was unknown outside Japan where he occupied a somewhat reclusive, legendary status. He was the progenitor of a true theatre of the body, which was inspirational for Mishima, the most physically obsessed writer of his time. He also inspired Eikoh Hosoe, who applied principles of theatre to his photographs in a way unknown in the West.

Hosoe began a collaboration with Hijikata, photographing him in performance outside the studio, often with other dancers, his head hooded in black and with flowers sprouting from his body. In 1960 Hosoe held an exhibition of his nudes of Hijikata and other dancers at a small gallery in Tokyo. Mishima wrote an essay for the catalogue, in which he spoke of a crisis between the classics and the avant-garde. Mishima viewed Hijikata's performance as heretical and seductive.

Hosoe and Hijikata worked together on a film, *Navel and Atomic Bomb* (1960) on a beach in Chiba. Hosoe combined nuclear imagery with a demonic presence from Hijikata, as the dancer walked from the sea to steal the navel of a child. The symbolic loss of innocence and sense of origin was explicit.

In his first book, *Man and Woman* (1961), Hosoe sequenced his photographs as a performance. At the start the models wore black leotards like dancers and they used fish, fruit and flowers as props. The gravure printing intensified the high contrast of the black and white imagery. As the sequence progressed, the bodies became more abstracted to reveal the curve of a breast, the line of an arm, or the shape of an oiled back. A woman's head appeared beneath the arm of a man, as if detached, in a gesture that only dance could have generated. The duality between male and female, between white and dark shapes, moved to a final, minimal form at the point of two touching breasts and the suggestion of inevitable human fusion. The essential contrast was between the female breast and the classical male torso, photographed like a fragment of an Apollonian figure. The sequence creates a pattern of restructuring and symbolic, biological healing. Hosoe was not examining the body in isolated, iconographic postures, but in active union.

Hosoe returned to the beach in Chiba with Hijikata to work on a further sequence, *Embrace*. Accidentally, at the time, he found a copy of Bill Brandt's book, *Perspectives of Nudes* (1961), which had just been published in London. Brandt had changed the potential of the nude for ever by both fragmenting and abstracting details of the body into pure, sculptural form which was heightened through the distortions of the lens. The site of many of Brandt's nudes was a beach. Hosoe knew he could not continue his series and left the photographs for nearly ten years. When he returned to *Embrace* he worked in the studio with dancers, including Hijikata, and continued to direct the performance of the male/female union, contrasting the softened, whitened female form with the darker, muscular tension of the male. He took his sense of the abstracted, fragmented body to the extreme. The photographs were not sculptural in a detached sense, but were full of the density of flesh with great tactile qualities; tendons and veins are stretched and fingers dig into soft, human surfaces. Mishima wrote an introduction to the book *Embrace* (1970) in which he described the lyrical whiteness. Mishima and Hosoe were joined in their common admiration for Hijikata.

Hijikata was the youngest child of a large family living in a country district in the far north of Japan. In his childhood imagination it was a landscape inhabited by the demons and spirits. From an early age Hijikata had lived among physical extremes. Mishima was his opposite, for he was from an established Tokyo family. His literary imagination had been nurtured in refined isolation. Mishima saw in Hijikata a physicality that extended beyond the surface of his body to his psychology as a man of action rather than a man of words.

Having seen some of Hosoe's first photographs of Hijikata, Mishima requested that Hosoe be commissioned to photograph him for a portrait to be included in a book of essays. Mishima asked that Hosoe photograph him as he had photographed Hijikata. He wanted to project himself with a similar physical presence. Mishima's physical transformation then became an exercise of the will, as if the size and tension of his muscle was a measure of his resolution.

Mishima astounded the world by his suicide in 1970. He had courted the Western press through a series of sensational postures, all of which appeared in contradiction to his prolific commitment to literature. He adopted many identities as if to disguise his extraordinary literary gifts, or to balance literary practice with intense physical action. He trained at *kendo*, body-building, piloted a jet fighter, played in gangster movies and started a private army. The manner of his death together with these various activities distracted commentators from the sublime quality of his prose and the substance of his

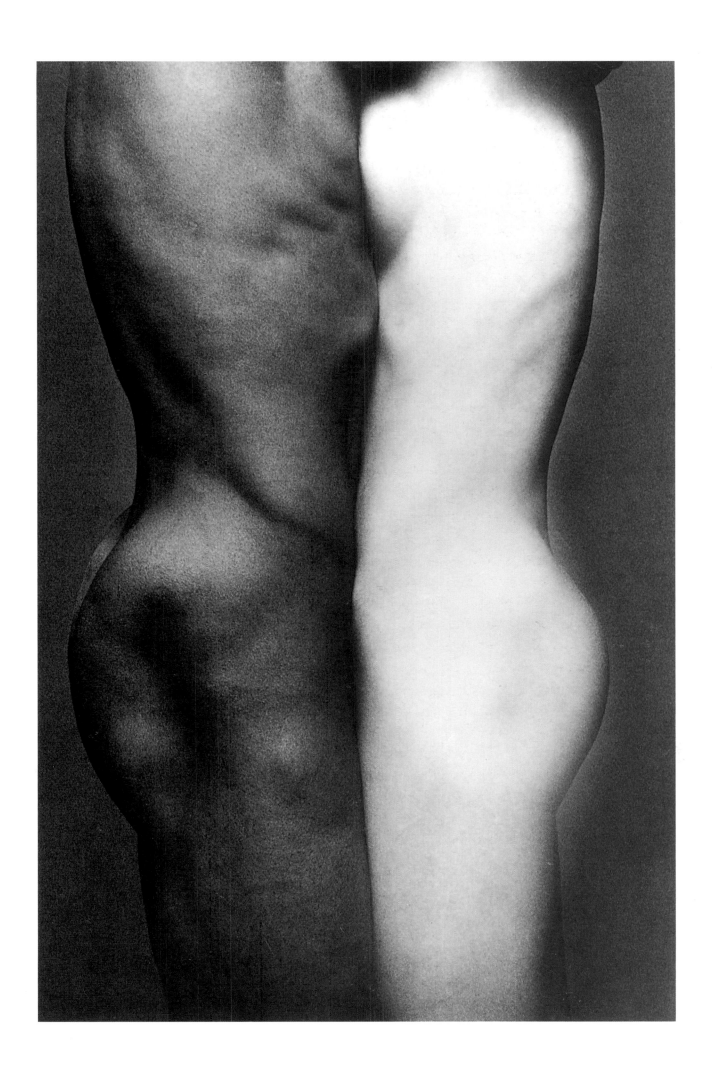

Eikoh Hosoe, from *Embrace*, 1971

work, which in retrospect reveals that his *seppuku*, ritual suicide, was almost inevitable. For Mishima a theatre of the body was an essential arena in which he could overcome all the ruptures and divisions to which he was vulnerable. Even in his most extravagant postures there was a philosophical premise that gesture or action of integrity was valid in itself whatever the outcome, a belief which was described as 'the nobility of failure'.* The gesture was infinitely more valuable than the thought.

Mishima is not a symbol of post-war Japan, nor of modern Japanese literature, though he has cast himself as an iconic figure. He most clearly represents the victim of history, a man caught in mid-century, between cultures and between the polar opposites of pre- and post-war Japan. He became an adult as the Emperor lost his divinity. His life is a series of contradictions, sexually, creatively and finally historically.

When Hosoe arrived for his first appointment to photograph Mishima, the writer was sunbathing in the garden of his rococo house. His father was watering the garden with a hose. Having been granted the freedom to photograph Mishima as he chose, Hosoe placed him on a marble zodiac in the garden and wrapped him in the hose. Immediately Mishima was placed against his own symbolic background. His physical tension was increased by the suggestion of the bondage which ensnared him. He was a trapped man as if enthralled by a private, masochistic world. Mishima and Hosoe became conspirators in this personal act of theatre. Mishima loved the photograph. For several months in 1961 and 1962 they worked together on a volume of work entitled *Barakei* (*Killed by Roses*, 1963), which was a cumulative photographic portrait, a morbid, erotic exploration, which can now be seen as another step in the rehearsal for Mishima's death. It is not a document but an exercise in artifice, with an entirely theatrical convention.

In the most famous photographs of writers, those of Baudelaire by Carjat and of Mayakovsky by Rodchenko, there is a sense that the writers are caught in some momentum that is propelling them to their subsequent destinies; Baudelaire to madness and Mayakovsky to suicide. It may be the knowledge that we ourselves project into the photographs, but they appear like men who have seen something beyond our imagination. We can look directly into their eyes. Hosoe's portrait of Mishima with a rose to his mouth in *Barakei* is a concentrated image of lyricism balanced by menace and eroticism. Mishima's physical power is evident in the line of his shoulder. He looks more like a dancer than a writer. He may have already begun to measure the time until his death.

Mishima had written obsessively about death and about *seppuku* in particular, just as he repeatedly glorified muscle and external, physical form. *Seppuku* conformed to traditional codes, and it also involved the penetration of the exterior form, the literal slashing of the body. His most violent passages are explorations of the moment of penetration. In *Homba* (*Runaway Horses*, 1969), his hero, Isao, seated on a clifftop, plunges the blade in as the sun rises, so mingling the sun's rays with the colour of blood. Mishima has also described the dissection of an animal in which the layers of the body are systematically stripped back in cold, anatomical exploration. These descriptions, however violent or explicit, contain a sense of inadequacy. The gulf between the language and the

*Ivan Morris, *The Nobility of Failure*, Secker and Warburg, London, 1975.

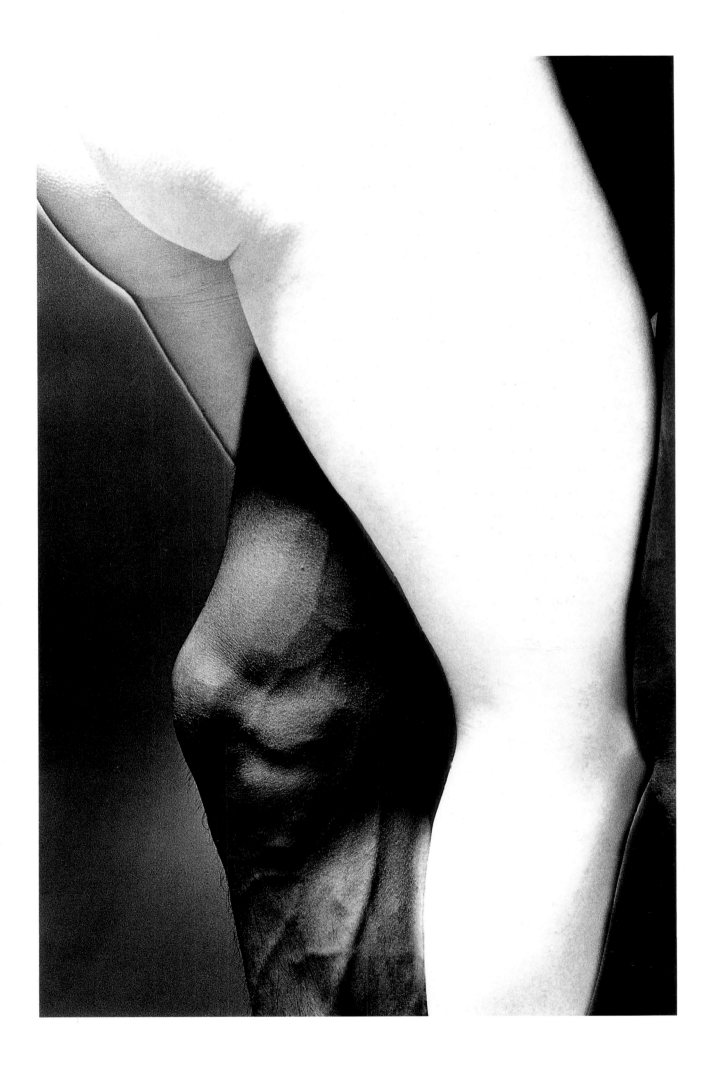

Eikoh Hosoe: from *Embrace*, 1971

Above and opposite Eikoh Hosoe: from *Embrace*, 1971

Following spreads Eikoh Hosoe: from *Embrace*, 1971; Yukio Mishima, from *Barakei (Killed by Roses)*, 1963.

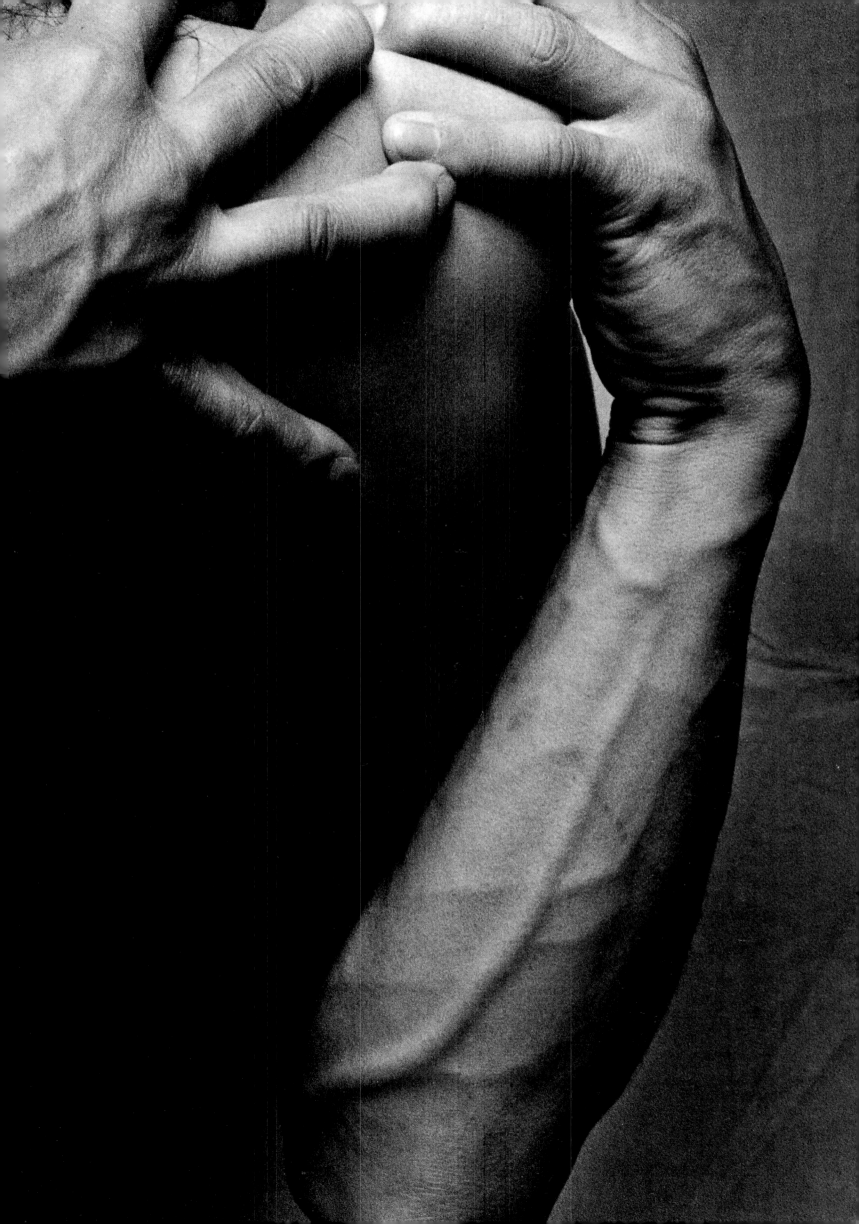

experience remains; so too does the division between the will or the interior force of the imagination and the exterior form of the body. Mishima was seeking some reconciliation between the two. He felt that ultimately, language was corrosive.

Mishima's adoption of the cult of the body was paralleled by his admiration for classical Greece and Rome and worlds of idealised physicality. As he asserted his Japanese identity, he drew fervently from Western tradition. With the Occupation of post-war Japan came the American cult of bodybuilding. The gymnasiums provided an opportunity for Japanese young men to transform their bodies to match idealised American proportions, to literally adopt the superior physique of their conquerors. Mishima frequented the gyms in search not only of the satisfaction of vanity, but to realise the harmony between the body and his interior world. In an introduction to a book on Japanese bodybuilders, *Taido* (*The Way of the Body*, 1966), there is a little-known essay by Mishima in which he wrote:

> Even in Japan today, where to outward appearances Westernization seems to have pervaded the land, the wisdom of ancient Greece – that of recognizing the supreme human worth of an equilibrium of spirit and body beneath the sun, that of investing the body, together with the spirit, with cultural value as something beautiful, noble, and at the same time, both immanent and transcendent – this wisdom has been completely forgotten. And in this way, thoughtless, we are rushing headlong towards fragmentation, fractionalization, and specialization, in short towards the dehumanizing of the human being that is the inevitable trend of industrialization.*

Mishima's fear of the industrial age lay in the fragmentation that was counter to his ideal of human equilibrium. The desire for perfect integration of body and spirit, or the reassembly of the whole man, was intensified in a writer who had contemplated total annihilation in 1945 at the age of twenty. In 1945 Mishima wrote what he assumed would be his final novel, *Chusei* (*The Middle Ages*), in which his fifteenth-century hero dies in battle at the age of twenty-four. His reading at the time was dominated by *Hagakure*, the treatise on *samurai* ethics, and by the two novels of Cocteau's protégé, Raymond Radiguet, who had died in 1923 at the age of twenty. He was experiencing the expectation of premature death at the same time as he was fully acquiring his facility as a writer.

While Mishima's desire for action was exercised in the gyms or the *kendo* training, he also turned to the *Noh* theatre with an almost religious veneration. The *Noh* theatre was a traditional form that he revitalised and assisted to preserve in the face of overwhelming Westernisation. Mishima's *Noh* plays were translated and published in the West in 1957. He suggested that adaptations of the plays in the United States should freely relocate the dramas, even considering Central Park in New York as a location. However traditional the form of *Noh*, the plays had potential beyond Japan. The action and language of *Noh* were also in perfect balance.

Mishima used a *Noh* stage as the set when filming his story *Yukoku* (*Patriotism*,

*English language edition of *Taido*: Tamotsu Yato, *Young Samurai, Bodybuilders of Japan*, Weatherhill, Tokyo, 1967.

Opposite Eikoh Hosoe: Yukio Mishima, from *Barakei (Killed by Roses)*, 1963

released in the US as *Rites of Love and Death*, 1961). The story referred to a military coup, the Ni Ni Roko Incident of 1936, a failed attempt to restore the Emperor as head of the Imperial Army. In the film, Mishima, playing the role of a young officer, commits *seppuku* on the *Noh* stage wearing only an officer's cap and a loin-cloth. The film was so vivid that audiences fainted in Tokyo and Paris when it was first screened in 1966. The film was punctuated by frames of language in which English phrases in Mishima's own hand floated over the surface of the screen, explicitly defining the duality of language and action.

Mishima's desires to act out his fantasies, not only to describe them, were realised through his friendship with Hijikata. According to Hijikata's widow, Akiko Motofuji, Mishima came to the dancer's studio many times to change himself into a dancer or to act out a physical role. The collaboration with Hosoe on *Barakei* was a similar act. However narcissistic this form of phototheatre became, Hosoe insists that Mishima was in fact a shy man and that the creation of *Barakei* was indeed a great challenge to him. It was an audacious act of self-exposure, in which the true elements of his imagination, sin and death beneath rococo glory, were enacted and so given substance that literature could not acquire. *Barakei* begins where Mishima's writing ends.

The theatricality of Mishima's house provides a sense of backdrop to the work. He sits at the marble top of a table, naked save for a loin-cloth, and struck by a brilliant arrow of light. Then, with his muscles glowing he stretches in Levi jeans across a stone seat. His figure is merged with Renaissance paintings with which in reproduction form he surrounded himself. At one point the theatre is explicit as a scenery painter was hired to produce a painted background of a forest and Mishima stands like St Sebastian against a tree trunk awaiting martyrdom. Guido Reni's painting of St Sebastian had been an important erotic cue for Mishima in adolescence. In his introduction to *Barakei* he described himself as a 'shadow in a time-machine'.

The book in its three different editions (1963, 1971, and 1985) reflects the scale of its ambition. The production on each occasion was monumental. A second edition was planned for publication in 1970 and Mishima worked on it with the graphic designer Tadanori Yokoo. The book, bound in black velvet, is enclosed in a case of white cloth with red characters. The case opens out to reveal a reclining naked Mishima sprouting roses beneath Hindu deities of reincarnation, in a design of almost psychedelic colour of the late Sixties. Yokoo's graphics exaggerate Mishima's muscle against the ocean and a blood-red sun. To open the book and the white case is in itself a ritual act. The sense of performance is extended to the viewing and turning of the pages by their sheer scale.

Mishima had planned that this production should be published in 1970 and everything was prepared for the month in which he died. The structure of the book was divided into five sections beginning with Sea and Eyes, followed by Eyes and Sins, Sins and Dreams, Dreams and Death, then finally Death. His plan was that it should appear with his suicide. On hearing of his death, however, Hosoe stopped publication to avoid surrounding the book with the sensationalism attached to Mishima's *seppuku*. The book eventually appeared the following year.

Opposite and following pages Eikoh Hosoe: Yukio Mishima, from *Barakei (Killed by Roses)*, 1963

Tadanori Yokoo had designed a remarkable poster for Mishima in 1969 when the writer was directing a production of *Chinzei Hachiro Tametomo* at the Kokuritsu Gekijo, the National Theatre in Tokyo. The poster, in Yokoo's *ukiyo-e* style included a clifftop scene with sword and blood. After Mishima's death the play was presented as a *Bunraku* puppet play for which Yokoo designed a new poster based on the original design over which a curtain of dark tones was dropped to symbolise his mourning. Theatre and design had become extensions of personal loss, not examples of literary or aesthetic style. The theatre of Mishima's life was pervasive.

Sacrifice overshadows *Barakei* and leaves a sense of Mishima's loss. He was at odds with his time and appeared to have lost his balance so that a darkness dominates his world, broken only occasionally by flashes of light as in the photographs themselves. The culmination of Mishima's theatre of the body was clearly death, which created a curious legacy for the society from which he had departed. A public that was not engaged in his literature was left only with a legend in the pose of a martyr and with his stinging accusations that the nation had lost its way and become drunk with prosperity.

Almost exactly as Mishima's era closed, a new theatre of the body, full of historical implication, emerged. In 1970, the year of both Mishima's death and the Japanese economic triumph of the Osaka Expo, Issey Miyake established his design studio in Tokyo. He had returned from Paris and the riots of 1968, and from New York. He had witnessed Europe in turmoil and the rock culture of America with its language of icons. A photograph of Issey Miyake taken that year, shows him sitting on the beach in Rio de Janeiro in a T-shirt of his own design. It forms a second skin decorated with the motifs of traditional Japanese tattoos. In place of the demonic or female faces of a *yakuza*'s (gangster) tattoo are the faces of Jimi Hendrix and Janis Joplin, to whose memory Miyake had dedicated his designs, as he did a year later with Marilyn Monroe. They appear at the beginning of his first book, *East Meets West* (1978).

Issey Miyake was a fabric expert and he intended to develop fabrics for the fashion houses. The Japanese textile industry was confident and the economic miracle revealed all the signs of accelerated growth. Tadanori Yokoo designed the textile pavilion at Osaka which was a dramatic symbol of an edifice under radical transformation. Out of a sweeping roof, curved like that of a temple or an old farm house, jutted a futurist structure in scarlet under scarlet scaffolding. The scaffolding echoed the designs of the traditional fences at the edge of the fields on which the rice straw was dried. Perched on the horizontals were the forms of large black crows, and the moulded bodies of construction workers in the postures of intense activity. It was a symbol of infinite growth, balanced between tradition and innovation.

Miyake's designs appeared in 1970 under the title *Peeling Away to the Limit*. His irregularly shaped fabrics were described by the architect Arata Isozaki:*

Breaking all of the rules, his pieces of material were merely clinging to the body. Moreover each piece was stripped away one after another until the body itself was in

*Arata Isozaki, 'What are Clothes? . . . A Fundamental Question', Issey Miyake, *East Meets West*, Heibonsha, Tokyo, 1978.

Opposite Tadanori Yokoo: poster for Tatsumi Hijikata, 1989 (103 × 72.8cm)

Tadanori Yokoo: poster for the *Kabuki* play, *Chinzei Hachiro Tametomo*, directed by Yukio Mishima,
Kokuritsu Gekijo (National Theatre), Tokyo, 1969 (103 × 72.8cm)

Tadanori Yokoo: poster for the *Bunraku* play, *Chinzei Hachiro Tametomo*, Kokuritsu Gekijo
(National Theatre), Toyko, 1970 (103 × 72.8cm)

full view. The result, in a way sadistic, was to take the body and the clothing away from each other, reducing their relationship to a minimum.

Miyake was exercising the art of reduction. By reducing the garment to a single piece of cloth, he wished to grant the body some sense of release not constriction. He refers to the French designer of the Twenties and Thirties, Madeleine Vionnet, who cut fabric in order to accommodate the body in movement. While he absorbed European fashion he also reasserted Japanese tradition by adopting native Japanese styles like *sashiko* quilting, *tanzen* robes and *shijira-ori*, the indigo-blue, woven cloth. This involved a movement back to the fundamentals of working clothes for farm people and to the classic unit of the *kimono*. Miyake was simultaneously developing design for the next decade while reinforcing the identity of the past. He was returning to history as he mapped the future. In the eight years from the founding of the Miyake Design Studio (1970) to the publication of *East Meets West*, Issey Miyake astounded the industry, both East and West, and transcended the labels of 'Japanese' and 'designer'. He resisted the attribution of the collective national title 'Japanese' by the West, which suffered the illusion that Japanese creative forces were somehow a homogenous entity. He had moved beyond the idea of design as an applied art to a dimension which resonated beyond his time and beyond Japan. Commentators attributed a philosophical dimension to Issey Miyake's designs. 'Body is to spirit, As cloth is to body', was stated on the invitation to an Issey Miyake fashion show on an aircraft carrier in the Hudson River in the early Eighties. Miyake was championed by philosophers, anthropologists, social academics, politicians and the international art world. They found in his work more than garments; they found an attitude of release and a sense of their bodies as active agents.

Whereas Mishima was a man torn apart by his duality, by the ruptures between East and West, Miyake was discovering a resolution. He was completing a circle and addressing a global culture of the future.

Tadanori Yokoo was inspired by Issey Miyake, as he had been inspired in a contrasting manner by Mishima. 'Issey Miyake's designs have gone beyond the limits of fashion to become the very essence of imagination itself . . . Just knowing that I am of the same generation stimulates my own imaginative powers,'* he said. Of Yokoo, Miyake said he was 'the Utamaro of his generation'. Yokoo collaborated with Miyake frequently and to this day he still designs the invitations to Issey Miyake shows. In addition to the graphics, Yokoo worked on print designs for Miyake fabrics, and this was extended to a major body of textile designs by Yokoo.

The most surprising collaboration appeared in Miyake's book *Bodyworks* (1983), entitled 'Tadanori Yokoo on Japanese Double Suicides'. A sequence of twelve colour photographs, shot by Toru Kogure under the direction of Yokoo, featured a series of suicides using boats and water. The narrative, like a short film, returns in each image to the movement of cloth, crumpled in the snow, flapping in the wind, or floating in the water. The suicide tale is established by cloth alone. There are no bodies in the

*Issey Miyake, *Bodyworks*, Shogakukan, Tokyo, 1983.

entire sequence. In an astonishing twist on Miyake's relationship between body and cloth, Yokoo suggested a concept of 'no body'. He created the presence of the body through its very absence.

Yokoo focused on the body as a subject for his painting to which he turned with increasing commitment in the Eighties. Like Robert Mapplethorpe in New York, he developed a fascination with the American bodybuilder, Lisa Lyon, who served as an icon of the liberated woman for the Japanese. Her physical presence suggested a previously unknown power. Yokoo not only painted her or drew her as she 'pumped up', but used her as the subject of video, a medium to which he was applying his graphic skills. He produced a video portrait of her, *Adept Arcana* (1985) with great technical virtuosity, in which he explored a multiplicity of video possibilities. The essential imagery of *Adept Arcana* was Lisa Lyon in a series of statuesque poses on mountain tops or by the ocean, transformed through an intense colour range, amidst the elements of fire and water. She appears at one point as a divine warrior wielding a Japanese sword. The music from Wagner's *Lohengrin* adds to the sense of a hybrid operatic epic, in which her body fulfils heroic poses, reminiscent of Leni Riefenstahl but shot through a psychedelic spectrum.

One of Yokoo's heroic paintings of the time, *Death of a Man or Portrait of Yukio Mishima with R. Wagner* (1983), linked Mishima's body with four painted heads of Wagner. Mishima stands with his arms bound above him to a tree, pierced by black arrows, with his head thrown back gazing at the heavens, as if in contemplation. The image travelled circuitously from Guido Reni's painting of St Sebastian, to a literal reconstruction of the painting, with Mishima as the model, photographed by Kishin Shinoyama only weeks before the writer's death, which in turn was painted by Yokoo. Actual bones are applied to the surface of this painting, which now hangs in Yokoo's house. It was a monumental work establishing Yokoo's sense of personal iconography. The canvas acts as a stage where his heroes converge from out of history.

By 1982, Issey Miyake's design had appeared on the cover of *Artforum* in New York, in a critical arena beyond the fashion world. The model on the cover wore a polished rattan bodice woven with bamboo, which followed the contours of her body. The editorial of the issue referred to the dialogue with images from the past and future:

Issey Miyake's jacket is a paraphrase of light samurai practice armor, which was made of bamboo and often decorated with designs that doubled as a scoring system (fencing defeats could be counted by the number of pierce marks). It is also a metaphor for a certain relationship to nature. The outfit is a contemporary second skin — its bodice is both cage and armor, lure and foil. The artificial shoulders of this 'iron butterfly' evoke the assertiveness and weaponry of a pioneer — woman — space-invader. Eastern and Western, a picture of fashion — she is a legend.*

Divine warriorship also existed in Miyake's vocabulary and echoes through the theatre of the body. Miyake's reductive process continued from the armour to a female

*Ingrid Sischy and Germano Celant, *Artforum*, New York, February 1982.

Test shots by Masayoshi Sukita for poster
for *Tradition et Nouvelles Techniques*, Paris, 1983.
Art director and graphic designer – Eiko Ishioka;
torso designer – Issey Miyake.

breastplate, replicating the contours of a woman's torso. The framing of the body had gone further than the framing by the rectangle of the photograph. The body had again become literally fragmented. The echoes of this 'second skin' were those of an ancient history with suggestions of a classical world, where the ideas of human form reflected those of a rational equilibrium. Miyake had peeled back all the layers and was left with the body itself.

By the end of the Eighties Miyake had entered into an extensive collaboration with the photographer Irving Penn in New York. Penn took Miyake's reductive principles to another extreme, abstracting the organic forms of Miyake's design against a pure, white background. Miyake published his work with Penn in 1988 and at the same time staged a great exhibition in Paris at the Musée des Arts Décoratifs. His clothes were displayed on manikins constructed out of wires and cables. The image was of the robotic body, or of the structure beneath the skin, and it was universal. The title of the exhibition consisted of two syllables, 'A Ūn'. 'A' represented the source and 'Ūn' represented a return to the source. It was a statement of dialogue and unity, an acceptance and resolution of duality.

Opposite Eiko Ishioka: offset poster for *Tradition et Nouvelles Techniques*, Paris, 1984. Torso designer – Issey Miyake; photograph – Masayoshi Sukita (103 × 72.8cm).

Tradition et Nouvelles Techniques

(12 Graphistes Japonais) 22 Octobre–15 Novembre 1984   Les Ateliers 48, rue Saint-Sabin 75011 Paris   Design par Eiko Ishioka, Imprimé au Japon par Toppan Printing Co., Ltd.   Ministère de la Culture/Délégation aux Arts Plastiques·Toppan Printing Co., Ltd.

DESIGN PAR EIKO ISHIOKA · PHOTOGRAPHIE PAR T. KITA.

Irving Penn: Issey Miyake design, 1988

Tsutomu Wakatsuki: Issey Miyake design, from *A Ūn* exhibition, Musée des Arts Décoratifs, Paris, 1988

3

THE THEATRE OF
REVOLT

THE INFECTIOUS NATURE of revolt characterised the Sixties as it does the Nineties. Paris, Prague, London, Chicago, Washington, Tokyo and other cities appeared locked in the same collective demonstration. Imagery ricocheted across the world. Girls offered flowers at the tips of bayonets during the anti-Vietnam march on the Pentagon in October 1967, just as a single young Chinese man stood in the path of the oncoming tanks approaching Tiananmen Square in 1989. Youth flaunted its innocence in the face of the military, resulting in visual imagery that could be translated on every continent, so fuelling the epidemic of revolt. By the summer of 1968 Mayor Daley's police had savagely beaten young Americans gathering in Chicago, and had been seen to do so on televisions across the world. In the Western world and Japan, youth was united with a shared popular music, a shared iconography of heroes, and a common opposition to the untenable nature of United States involvement in Vietnam.

The war in Asia directly implicated Japan on account of the terms of the revision of the United States–Japan Security Treaty in 1960, which inflamed mass opposition at the very start of the decade. Haneda airport in Tokyo became overcrowded with United States military charter flights, which were granted free use of the airport under the terms of the treaty. American bases throughout Japan and Okinawa formed the skeleton of US power in South-East Asia. They became the obvious focus of opposition to the Vietnam War itself. The development of the new Narita airport in the farming district of Sanrizuka outside Tokyo became an opposition cause allied to the anti-Vietnam movement. The farmers originally received support from the Japanese Communist and Socialist parties, but then gained an alliance with the radical Left student movement. The war in Vietnam effectively politicised a generation, who soon began to employ the guerrilla techniques of a peasant resistance movement in response to the riot police at the airport, resulting in battles on an epic scale. The climax of this struggle between 1967 and 1971 coincided with the climax of commercial and industrial strength which Japan wished to demonstrate to the world through the Osaka Expo of 1970.*

The Japanese student movement of the Left, *Zengakuren*, had been founded in 1948 as a democratic opposition to any post-war re-emergence of Fascism. At the end of the Fifties there was a split between the student movement and the Communist party, though the JCP remained highly influential with control of many student bodies. The radical Left included Maoists, Trotskyites and Anarchists and there were frequent internal struggles and inter-factional battles.†

The student revolt began to reach a peak in January 1968 at Tokyo University, resulting in a strike at the Medical School in March of that year over conditions of unpaid internship, which escalated to bring the university to a standstill for several months. A parallel revolt developed at the nearby Nihon University, which was a private institution, over embezzlement of funds and donations to the ruling Liberal-Democratic party. In 1969 the disparate student factions were united as *Zenkyoto*, the All-Japan Federation of Joint Struggle Committees.

At Tokyo University a hard core of the students occupied a central hall on the campus from November 1968 to January 1969, when despite the taking of hostages, the students were driven out under storm from 850 riot police. Mishima was said to have respected the determination of the students but regretted that none of them had demonstrated their commitment by acts of suicide.

In May 1969 Mishima was challenged by the students to a debate on the campus itself. The debate was an extraordinary event, as the values of pre-war Japan, with emphatic adoration of the institution of the Emperor by Mishima, collided head-on with the radical Left, who had been participating not simply in a violent local dispute, but in the wave of international revolt of their generation. Mishima also gained the opportunity to challenge his fearlessness in a situation that could have provoked violence. He went unaccompanied. 'If only you would speak the Emperor's name, I would gladly join hands with you,' he told them. He won respect for his courage but was ridiculed for his perceived anachronisms. He admired their defiance and extremism. The debate was published successfully and he granted the students half of the royalties. 'They probably used the money to buy helmets and Molotov cocktails. I bought summer uniforms for the *Tate-no-kai*, [his Shield Society]. All concerned are satisfied.'‡

The international opposition to the Vietnam War and the specific Japanese riots within the universities and out on the Sanrizuka plain created a climate of revolt and a language that also found expression in acts of artistic liberation. The force of rebellion released a storm of vitality. The demonstrations became cathartic forms of public theatre. In artistic terms the city was to become a stage, though the tear gas, batons and blood were real. History seemed more theatrical than theatre itself. History could coincide with the choreographed cinematic imagery of revolt so famously depicted by Sergei Eisenstein.

---

*Jon Halliday and Gavan McCormack, *Japanese Imperialism Today*, Penguin Books, Harmondsworth, 1973.

†Gavan McCormack, 'The Student Left in Japan', *New Left Review 65*, January–February 1971.

‡John Nathan, *Mishima*, Hamish Hamilton, London, 1975.

Two decades later, Tiananmen Square provided an international spectacle that seemed epic, even operatic, since the action was largely contained within a single arena. The reality of the savagery was hidden from the public on the morning after the bloodshed when the approach roads were literally draped with curtains, which concealed the activities of the 'stage hands' as they swept away the debris of the previous night. Then the government declared the play was over. Shuji Terayama, poet, dramatist, film-maker and creative genius of the late Sixties Tokyo underground, later announced in his *Manifesto* of 1975 that, 'The theatre is neither a set of factors nor a building. It is the ideology of a place where dramatic encounters are created . . . Any space can become theatrical space . . . Theatre is chaos.'

It is said that in May 1968 when the Paris students stormed the Odéon-Théatre de France (which was then under the direction of Jean-Louis Barrault), and occupied Barrault's office, on seeing a portrait of Antonin Artaud on the wall, they declared, 'He has stolen Artaud.'* Artaud, visionary poet and creator of the Theatre of Cruelty, was a hero of the counter-culture because of the vehemence of his attack on the conventions of theatre and on the values of the bourgeoisie, which he expressed for example in his essay on Van Gogh whom he described as an artist 'suicided by society'.

Through his theoretical writing Artaud defined principal distinctions between Western and Oriental theatre. In 1931 he had seen Balinese dance performed in an Indonesian temple constructed at the Colonial Exhibition at the Bois de Vincennes. He was overwhelmed by the possibility of a theatre established through a vocabulary of gesture rather than through the 'stuttering' of language that constituted Western drama. He wrote repeatedly about Oriental theatre in *The Theatre and Its Double* (1938) and incorporated it into his own sense of a revolutionary spectacle.

In the Sixties the legacy of Artaud not only touched the mood of the Paris streets, but his influence reached Japan, together with Lautréamont, Jean Genet, and the Marquis de Sade, whose *One Hundred Days of Sodom* was translated by Tatsuhiko Shibusawa. Artaud's idea of culture resonated in perfect synchronism with the time. It was 'an idea which is first of all a protest . . . A protest against the senseless constraint imposed upon the idea of culture by reducing it to a sort of inconceivable Pantheon. . . . A protest against the idea of culture as distinct from life.'†

Issey Miyake was working in Paris at the height of the riots in May 1968. He had left Japan to serve his apprenticeship in the French fashion houses and had been engaged in his own revolt since 1960 when he was a student at the Tama College of Fine Arts. A major international design conference had then relegated fashion design to a peripheral secondary status. His revolt was against an establishment that failed to understand that fashion, in contrast to the design of the couture houses, was a public expression. It was a social act. The Paris demonstrations deeply impressed him and forced him to question the possible response of design and the accompanying fashion industry to the public climate of revolt. He then went to America to discover in New York the role of pop culture through the visual language of such artists as Rauschenberg and Warhol. He returned to Japan to

*Martin Esslin, *Antonin Artaud*, Fontana, London, 1976.

†Antonin Artaud, *The Theatre and Its Double*, Grove Press, New York, 1958.

Opposite Eiko Ishioka: offset poster, Gallery Nippon, Toyko, 1968. Caption – Kazuko Koike;
photograph – Noriaki Yokosuka (103 × 72.8cm)

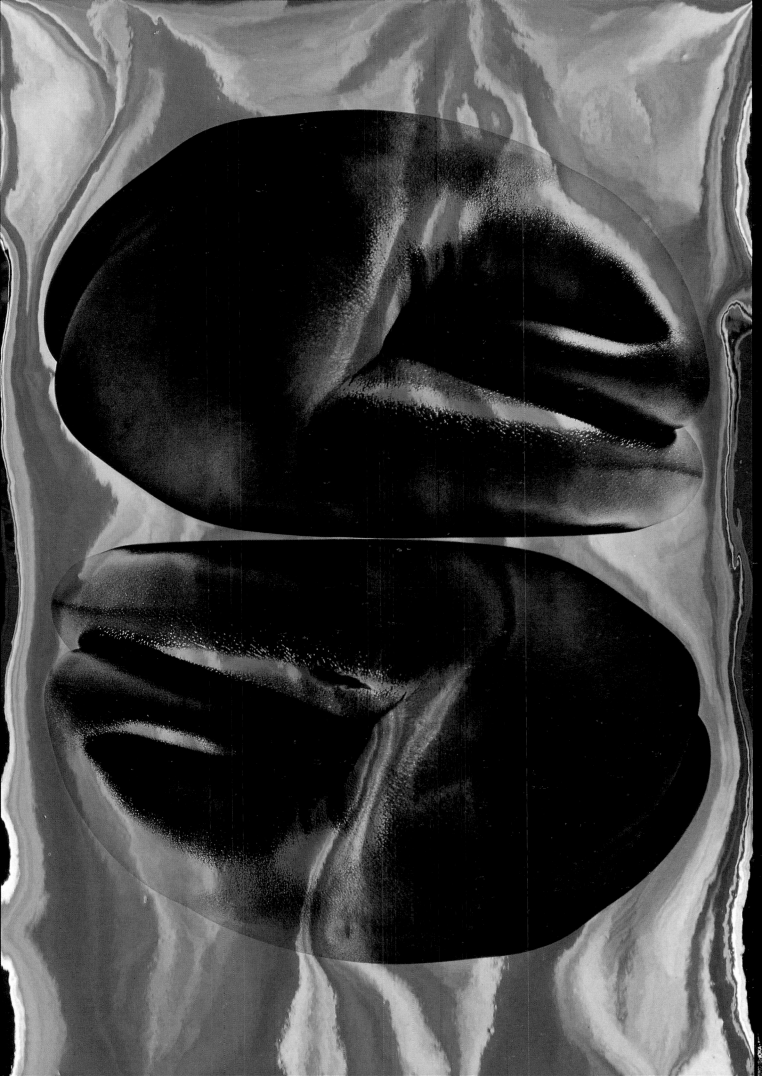

establish his own studio in 1970, having absorbed couture skills, the appropriation of mass culture into art, and the dynamic of rebellion.

In 1968, Eiko Ishioka, who had been a student at Tama with Issey Miyake and was to become the leading graphic designer and art director in Japan over the next decade, was invited by the Gallery Nippon in Tokyo to participate in a poster exhibition entitled 'War, Protest and Freedom'. The poster she designed, printed on silver metallic paper, portrayed two naked bodies folded like clenched fists under the caption 'Power Now', which accommodated all revolt – the politics of civil rights, the feminist movement, and the anti-war protest. Like Issey Miyake, Eiko Ishioka was following the path adopted by the most intelligent Japanese of her generation. She was absorbing the language of revolt, understanding the power of the slogan and its implication in mass culture, and then placing it in the heart of a Japanese context, where it would explode amidst a generation of Japanese youth ready to assert a new identity. Both Issey Miyake and Eiko Ishioka belonged to a generation that grew up in the aftermath of the war; Ishioka in Tokyo, the scene of the firebombing, and Miyake in Hiroshima. Their extraordinary ambition coincided with the transformation of Japan itself. Harnessing the energy of revolt was necessary for the creation of a new Japan.

For photographers, the sheer physicality and drama of revolt provided a valuable and graphic subject. Chaos on the streets was as photogenic as the spectacle of battle. Daido Moriyama, formerly Hosoe's assistant and the most influential of the young Japanese photographers of the time, recalls the culmination of 1968 in the Anti-War Day on 31 October, when the riots in the Shinjuku district of Tokyo were at their most intense. He remembers that the fighting between the students and the police became so heavy that the roar was displaced by a sense of silence and detachment; it was as if he was watching a silent newsreel of history. The experience of the spectacle was so strong that he returned to his work with the intention of creating photography that was as intense as what he had witnessed. One of his platforms at the time was the large-format magazine, *Provoke*, which he co-founded.

It was in this volatile climate that Shomei Tomatsu published his most strident books. Tomatsu had grown up close to the American base at Nagoya in the immediate post-war years. He witnessed a world of affluence within the base, which was inconceivable after the deprivations of the war years. The Occupation, he told me, coincided with his entering the adult world:

> The Occupation was the start of a new life for me. When I began to photograph I went back to the American bases. The military had left my neighbourhood and concentrated their forces elsewhere. The other bases, such as those at Yokota, Yokosuka, Sasebo and on Hokkaido and Okinawa, became the most significant places for me, places from which I could assess my own life.

Coupled with this fascination for life in the separate world of the bases was his frequent travel to Okinawa, where he found island communities of farmers and fishermen living with archaic values that once prevailed on the islands of Japan itself. He discovered an animistic culture in contact with the elements and full of physical exuberance amidst the great beauty and fecundity of the landscape. For Tomatsu, Okinawa fulfilled his own fantasy of 'Japan', or of a Japan that could never be. On Okinawa this fantasy existed beside the presence of the American bases. It was here that the clash of cultures was most explicit and this became the subject of his work.

In his book, *Okinawa* (1969), Tomatsu forced the juxtaposition of the American military – the wire fences, jeeps, bombers, hardware, combat cloth – into graphic conflict with the sheer physical density of the island and the poverty and simplicity of the lives of the islanders. Planes take off and land throughout the book. With the servicemen comes the secondary industry of sex and recreation, the bars and small hotels, where the islanders serve the alien occupying forces. Caught between the two sides are the local politicians mingling on the pages with the gatherings of the military hierarchy. Storming into the conflict come the armies of revolt. Under the banners 'Carry Away B52s From Okinawa' Tomatsu photographed the helmeted youths and their mass gatherings. Their banners are photographed against the Okinawa sky like a medieval army, marching in battle array against an impossible military machine.

Shinjuku, the epicentre of the Sixties revolt, was the subject of Tomatsu's other book of the time. *Oh Shinjuku!* (1969) was a violent and erotic homage to this extraordinary district of Tokyo. Shinjuku is centred around the enormous railway station and throughout the Eighties it has been the site of drastic redevelopment. Close to the station is a small maze of shops, noodle stalls and bars, representing an underworld in immediate proximity to the great department stores. In Shinjuku there is also the largest book store in the city, making it a natural meeting place for students. It is now one of the densest sites of teenage consumerism. The neon of Shinjuku is challenged by the television image on a giant, exterior screen, which continually broadcasts pop promotional videos. In the midst of this point of convergence is the district of Kabuki-cho, the territory of Shinjuku strip joints, *yakuza*, and bars. A closed, interior world of sex spreads out through its alleys. Beside Kabuki-cho is yet another self-contained quarter, the Golden Gai, a maze within a maze of two-storeyed wooden houses on a narrow grid, which serve as bars. It is a sealed world of old Tokyo, threatened by further redevelopment.

It was on these streets that Nagisa Oshima set his film, *Diary of a Shinjuku Thief* (1968). The main character in the film was played by the designer Tadanori Yokoo, who, in addition to his role as an actor, produced two posters for the film. Oshima portrayed an underworld culture, a street of crime as in Marcel Carné's *Les Enfants du Paradis* (1945), where the world of actors, artists and performers met the criminal underworld. This clandestine environment carried with it erotic currents, which became more prevalent in a climate of sexual liberation accompanying a theatre of revolt.

Shinjuku in 1968 demonstrated a shocking equation between the political violence on the streets, full of shouting and adrenalin, with an interior world of female forms and the enactment of a form of sexual theatre. While the exterior world appeared to be howling in a great clash of protest, behind the doors of Shinjuku, another form of tension, frequently voyeuristic, appeared to be heightened. The protests were ultimately expressed in two famous photographs by Tomatsu: one blurred image shows a single man running

Following spread Masahisa Fukase: Shinjuku, 1968, from *Homo Ludence*, 1971

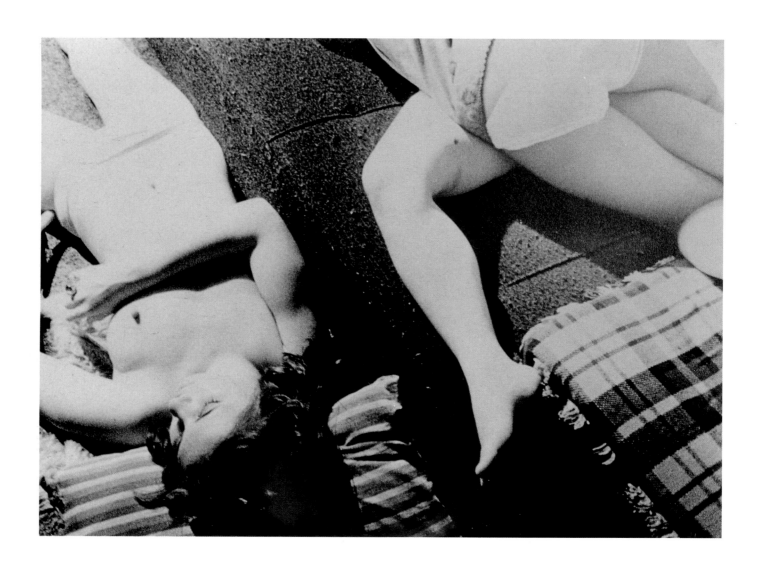

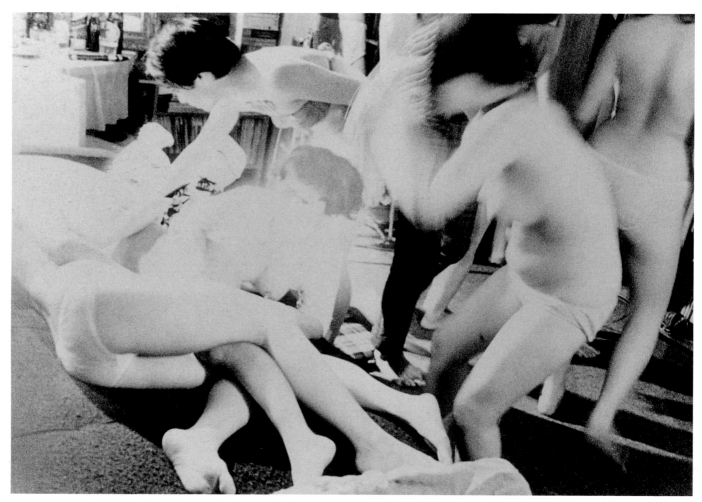

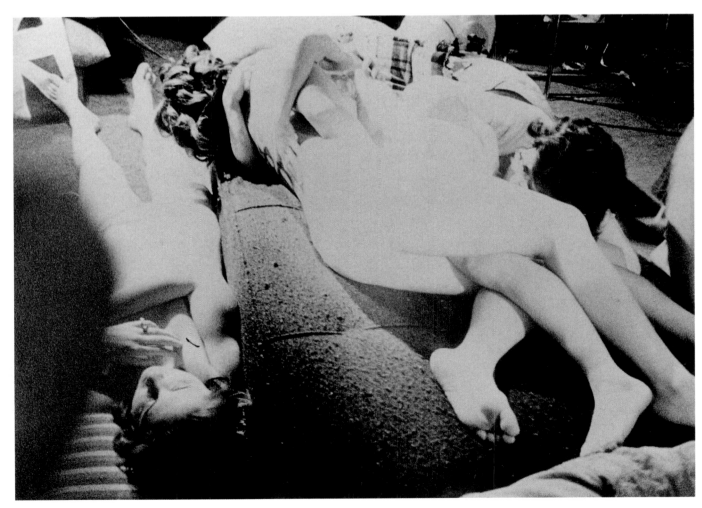

across the street, which is strewn with debris, and is caught in a gesture of hurling his missile, while another photograph shows an army of police lined up with their shields as if to receive the missile. Tomatsu had intensified the sense of the conflict by an act of simple reduction to the single figure in the midst of the chaos. There is a third photograph, which bridges the worlds of *Eros and Power*, as Tomatsu defined them. A girl's face contorts into a scream. On the ground beside her is a Molotov cocktail made from a Coca-Cola bottle. She is frozen in a silent scream.

The sexual and political frenzy was taken to a further extreme by the photographer Masahisa Fukase, during those chaotic days in Shinjuku. Several of his most abstract and graphic scenes of Shinjuku parties degenerating into orgies provide scenes of exhaustion as well as licentiousness. This work was included in his first book, *Homo Ludence* (1971) and at the first exhibition of Japanese photography at the Museum of Modern Art in New York in 1974. Fukase stretched the limit of what was possible to photograph, in a visual language that side-stepped the pornographic and which was as blurred and fragmented as the events depicted. Extracted from the imagery of the late Sixties, they now appear like signals of the last dance, the final collapse, or the symbolic morning after a party that went well out of control.

Many of the creative figures in Japan were associated in a common subversive culture of the period, which broke through the limitations or classifications of art. Film-makers, writers, photographers, dancers and designers shared common directions through collaboration. The most conspicuous figure of this fertile time was Shuji Terayama, who acted as a catalyst and exercised a multiplicity of talents. He had been recognised as a poet while still a student in the Fifties. At the start of the next decade he was working with the dancer, Tatsumi Hijikata and writing plays and essays on politics, gambling and boxing, a particular passion of his. In the boxing ring he evidently saw a conflict of great theatrical value. In 1967 he founded *Tenjosajiki*, a Laboratory of Theatre Play, with the designer Tadanori Yokoo, the director Yutaka Higashi, and the producer Eiko Kujo. The experimental theatre of *Tenjosajiki* drew strongly on elements of circus and the tradition of travelling players, with Yokoo acting as art director and designing the posters. Terayama described the first phase of *Tenjosajiki* as centred on the conflict between Japanese tradition and the contemporary reality, using mythological creatures like the snake-girl and the wolf-boy. They encouraged the participation of minority groups, the handicapped and homosexuals. Their first productions included *The Hunchback of Aomori* and *One Thousand and One Nights in Shinjuku*. Terayama acknowledged the influences of Lautréamont and Artaud on his theatrical subversion and declared a challenge on the conventions of realist theatre.

At the end of the Sixties he performed plays without actors, using instead students and workers who came on stage to read their letters and to describe their sexual problems. He began work writing and directing his film, *Throw Away Your Books, Let's Go Into the Streets* (1971), an assault on the family, sexual values, and discrimination in Japanese society. The film was anarchic and visually shocking with an extreme spectrum of colour. Terayama's images of the boxing ring, street theatre and sexual confession recur throughout. In 1969 he staged experimental productions in Frankfurt and Essen in Germany and the following year he worked at La MaMa in New York. Throughout the early Seventies his productions travelled extensively, frequently winning prizes. His schedule included productions in Nancy, Rotterdam, Amsterdam, Belgrade, in Munich during the 1972 Olympics, and on to Denmark, Poland and Iran, while simultaneously he continued work as a film director. His second feature film, *Pastoral Hide and Seek* (1974) was the official Japanese entry at the Cannes Film Festival. At the same time he was publishing numerous essays on the theory of theatre. His output was prolific and his energy took his work out of Shinjuku and Japan and into the international avant-garde. By the mid-Seventies he was still active in Tokyo and *Tenjosajiki*'s street performances, *Knock* (1975), involved the appearance of mysteriously dressed actors at the houses and workplaces of the unsuspecting people, resulting in several arrests in Tokyo. He remained engaged in a continual struggle with ideas of society and the State. Terayama's theatre coincided totally with the greater sense of revolt against the tight strictures of Japanese life, both within the family and within society at large. As a pioneer of the avant-garde, he also drew the support of Mishima, who used his influence and wealth not only in such gestures as funding his own fantasy army, the *Tate-no-kai*, but also in the patronage of those whose artistic audacity he endorsed. Terayama was a champion of the audacious gesture, at which Mishima was the prime exponent, and although his theatrical revolt coincided with that of the radical Left, like Mishima he was a writer who drew from literary influences beyond Japan, and who married them to his native traditions. However 'Japanese' his work in retrospect appears, his actual arena extended well beyond Japan itself.

In the final sequence of *Throw Away Your Books, Let's Go Into the Streets*, Terayama's nineteen-year-old hero addresses the viewer with accusations that curse Japan both for its insularity and for its absorption into the American machine. His rage is neither that of the Left nor that of the Right. It comes from a nihilism and displacement shared with the youth of the West:

> The white screen
> Who said 'everyone can be a world celebrity for fifteen minutes'?
> All that's left to show are these dozens of men
> disappearing with this film
> And this blank screen.
> I've got no home,
> I've got no country.
> There's no world for me.
> None of that existed for me from the start.
> Alone, without any family, only photographs count.
> With a photo in my hand I draw Auld Lang Syne,
> My Auld Lang Syne.
> When I was at school, I picked up a lizard in a park
> I put it in a Coca-Cola bottle and it became too large to get out,
> A lizard in a Coca-Cola bottle,
> You don't have the strength to get out, do you Japan?

93

Terayama also appropriated photography into his arsenal of media; he was attracted to the ritual of the photographer. He remembered the moments as a child when he smelt the magnesium of the primitive flash; it was a magical ritual not unlike that of a circus act or of a conjurer. His mother had warned him that each time he was photographed he would lose part of his shadow. When he eventually saw Michael Powell's film *The Tales of Hoffmann*, he was impressed by the image of a man who sold his shadow, which seemed to him to be exactly what happened when one was photographed. Photography provided the possibility of an arcane ceremony and became an extension of his theatre.

In the early Seventies he placed an advertisement in a Tokyo newspaper requesting the help of people who were prepared to be transformed in the studio. He acquired about three hundred amateur models who, together with members of *Tenjosajiki* who wanted to exercise their fantasies, became willing participants in a form of theatre he created in the studio. The scenes were often fetishistic and masochistic. Terayama prepared the props, allowed his subjects to indulge themselves and photographed them. He then printed the photographs as postcards on which he stuck old postage stamps, which often displayed imagery of fighter planes, imperial insignia and other emblems of pre-war or wartime Japan. He made up a postmark from Shanghai, stamped the photos and often inscribed poems or quotations on them. This series formed a family called *Les Gens de la Famille Chien-Dieu* which he exhibited in Tokyo in 1974 and published as a book the following year.

Photography became another form of encounter for him, 'In my work I want to organise an encounter with the imagination. Theatre consists of chance encounters. Encounters are all incidents, they are not planned. To provide the opportunity for these accidents or incidents, this is what I call creation.' Photography allowed him to disrupt reality and construct fiction. He had no interest in either photographic technique or in photographic 'truth'. He saw the medium as another means of revolt. 'Steal the shadows of others!' he declared and added in the same subversive spirit:

> Lizzie Borden took a camera
> Shot her father forty times
> When she saw what she had done
> She shot her mother forty-one.

The climax of the rebellion that occurred in Japan was executed by the dancer, Tatsumi Hijikata. On two consecutive days in October 1968 he performed his masterpiece, a dance lasting two hours entitled *Revolt of the Flesh* or *Tatsumi Hijikata and the Japanese*. He withdrew into preparation for almost a year, and in the final weeks he brought his body to a peak through fasting, exercise and a strict diet. It was a turning point in his life. He was thirty-nine years old.

Hijikata employed his whole range of technique, transforming himself, changing his sex and his age, as if he was contradicting the limitations of his own body. He stomped the ground like a flamenco dancer, he pirouetted in a dress, he jerked in spasms with a gilded phallus strapped to his naked body. He sacrificed a chicken, and he writhed like

Above and following spreads Shuji Terayama: from *Les Gens de la Famille Chien-Dieu,* 1975

リッチフィールドの
贋作雲井展
御時世を、迎合って騒がせ
ましたり、頼春として汚します時

ユーの刑すが安き
誹謗がどれほど
身に沁みましたことか。
できますならば今後
兄！と呼ばせて下さいな。
眞家の弟より

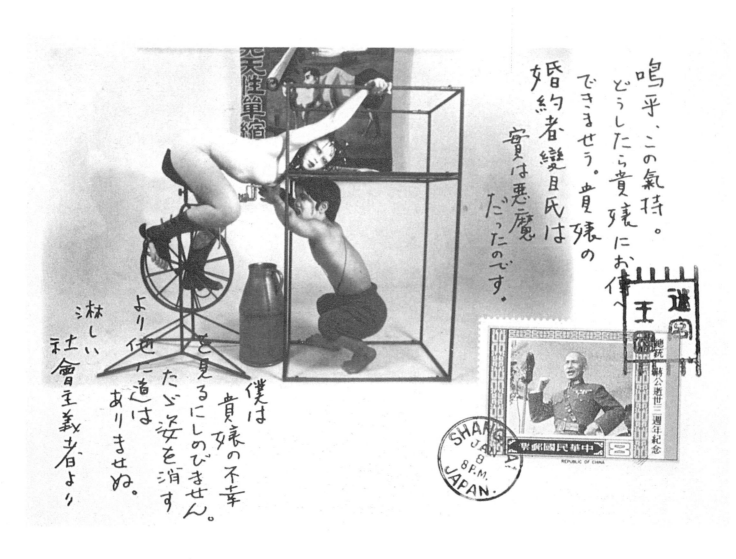

嗚呼、この氣持。
どうしたら貴嬢にお伸
できませう。貴嬢の
婚約者變目氏は
實は悪魔
だったのです。

僕は
貴嬢の不幸
を見るにしのびません。
ただ姿を消す
より他に道は
ありません。
淋しい
社會主義者より

票着せし
小包の中に
たごひとすじ
では
ありますが
正体不明の
黒髪のありましたことを
御報告いたします
馬器男拝

綴ります

小生ひたすら
一にラブしたので御在います

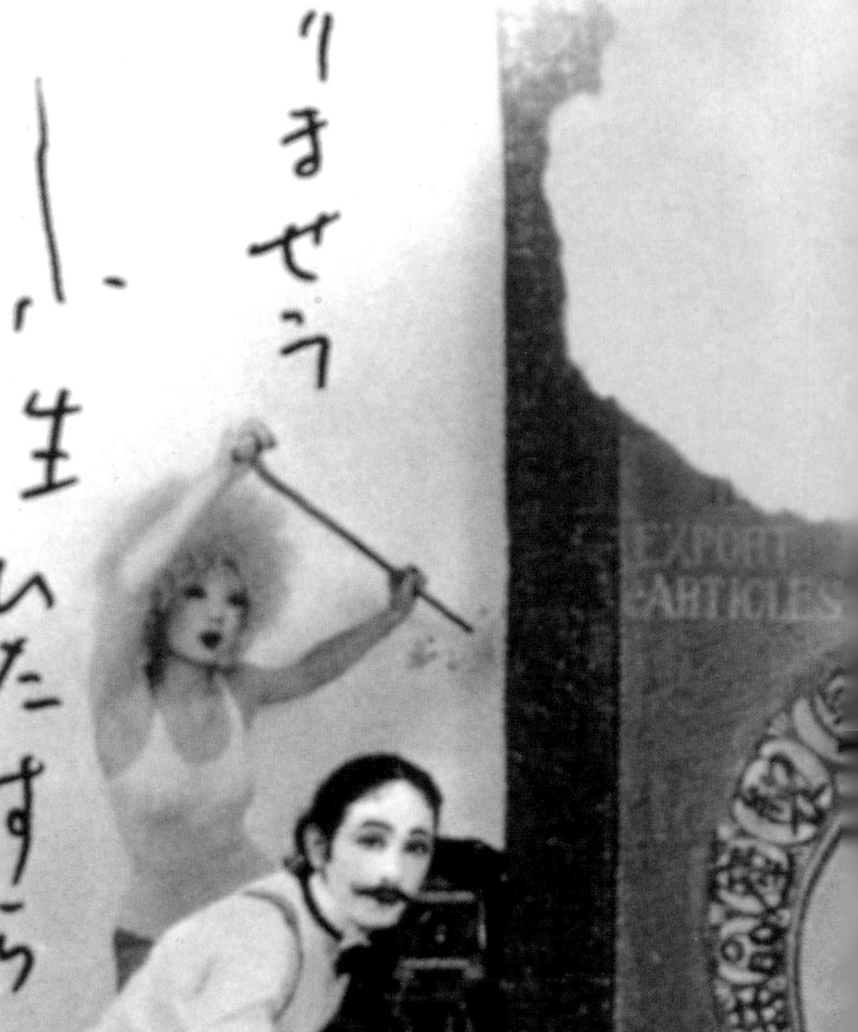

近視
大神博士
元

Above Eikoh Hosoe: Tatsumi Hijikata in *Honegami Toge Hotokekazura (Corpse Vine on Ossa Famine Ridge)*, 1970

a possessed shaman. It was a dance from neither East nor West. It had no precedent. It surfaced from deep within his memory as far back as his early childhood. His pupil Yoko Ashikawa said that as the performance progressed, he appeared to become younger. There was a crescendo as he was suspended, his naked body strung by ropes across the stage. It seemed like a moment of sacrifice, as if he was being torn apart.

Two years before his death I visited Hijikata at his studio. A lean, stooped man, his hair tied back and running down to his waist, he was charismatic. I could gain no indication of his real age, though he was in fact in his mid-fifties. When he projected an archive film of *Revolt of the Flesh* I had a sense not of watching a document from the Sixties, nor even from Japan. It was closer to a Central Asian or Siberian ceremony, maybe even an Indian initiation rite, filmed by some explorer half a century before. Hijikata had taken and absorbed influences from Spain, from the Neue Tanz from Germany, and married them with his native magic and the demons from the far north. His revolt went further than the prevalent nihilism of the time to mark a new beginning, the establishment of his own vocabulary, a true birth of *Butoh* dance, through which he could make the descent deep into his subconscious in polar opposite to Nijinksy's soaring, vertical ascent, seventy years before.

Later in an upstairs room in his studio, with a bare, polished floor and a low table, he sat and drank. He seemed to speak in chains of images, stringing together his associations, which at one point encompassed Joan Miró, Edvard Munch and Francis Bacon, out of which emerged an image of a scream. He then spoke of Artaud and mentioned that one of his most valued possessions was a tape of Artaud's scream from a banned French radio broadcast of 1948 (A poem for four voices, xylophone and percussion – *Pour en finir avec le jugement de Dieu*).

Whiskies followed and he leant across the table and suddenly seized a slab of ice, which in a second he smashed on the corner of the table. I sat respectfully silent then commented on the exquisite grain of the table. He responded by slowly withdrawing the cigarette from his mouth and purposefully stubbing it round and round into the table top. All notions of harmony or aesthetics that I might have harboured were burned up in a single gesture. When I rose to leave he bowed, then informally kissed me, endearingly not provocatively. Outside it was a hot summer night and the festival of Bon Odori was beginning. The streets of Meguro were lined with lanterns. Drums were beating. It was the last night of *Obon*, the feast of the dead. It is a night of rejoicing for the souls liberated from Buddhist hells into a state of celestial bliss, celebrated for centuries by wild dancing and the stomping of feet.

Following spread Tadao Nakatami: Tatsumi Hijikata in *Tatsumi Hijikata and the Japanese: Rebellion of the Body* or *Revolt of the Flesh*, 1968

4

THE THEATRE OF
THE STREET

THE HEAVY TILED roofs of the Tokyo houses spread across a great plain. Wires and aerials criss-cross the flat skyline. Seen from a train, the narrow alleys of the city form a skeleton map, from which the shopping centre or department store rise as neon punctuation marks on the horizon, in pink, orange, or lime green, the colours of a new sign language. The elevated highways, the tracks of the suburban train lines, and the overhead wires lead into the city centre, the electric axis from which Tokyo receives and dispatches its signals, where economic strategies are planned, markets rise and fall, television commercials are conceived, advertisements designed, and the image bank pours out its language. The axis is no longer the hub of Japan alone; its orbit now encompasses most of the globe. The city conforms to no preconceptions of either East or West. The façade is like that of a new city in a new century. Its history and collective memory are often well concealed. Tokyo is both an urban landscape of the future as if designed in comic strip, the obsessive reading matter of its inhabitants, and a shadowy world of the past, full of literary and cinematic allusion, echoing the Japan that the West has traditionally consumed. A city of many layers or many doors lurks behind the neon surface of its chaos. The wires that radiate out from its centre, its nervous system, connect it to the whole world.

The German film-maker, Wim Wenders, visited Tokyo in the early Eighties to discover what remained of the city he had experienced through the films of Yasujiro Ozu, who died in 1963 and whose work he treasured. In Wenders's own film *Tokyo-Ga* (1984), a homage to Ozu, he described his arrival:

> The more the reality of Tokyo struck me as a torrent of impersonal, unkind, threatening, yes, even inhuman images, the greater and more powerful became, in my mind, the images of the loved and ordered world of the mythical city of Tokyo that I knew from the films of Yasujiro Ozu ... Perhaps the frantically growing inflation

of images has already destroyed too much. Perhaps images at one with the world are already lost forever.*

Wenders then encountered his friend Werner Herzog, who was searching for pure, 'transparent' imagery that might correspond to his idea of civilisation. Tokyo seemed to represent an absence of such imagery for Herzog. 'You see,' said Herzog, 'when I look out from here, everything's all built up. Out there images are nearly impossible. You almost have to dig with a shovel like an archaeologist and simply look and see if anything's left to be found amidst the defamed landscape.'

Wenders understood Herzog's search for the 'transparent' image, but realised, 'the images I was searching for were only to be found down below, in the chaos of the city. In spite of everything, I couldn't help being impressed by Tokyo.'

In certain back streets of Tokyo I have found the mythical city for which Wenders searched. In Yanaka, the district of the great cemetery to the north of Ueno, in the east of the city, is an area of old wooden houses and temples, untouched by the war. Walking through the narrow streets, there is the smell of incense, the sound of children or a dog. Family life, straight out of Ozu, continues in a neighbourhood where there are still merchants making paper or printing with woodblocks. In proximity to the cemetery, bordered by the railway track, Yanaka is the territory squeezed between the lines of communication and the land of Edo ghosts.

In the Golden Gai, beside the Kabuki-cho of Shinjuku, are the small bars of the old city. It is a closed world of private drinking. The inhabitants of this enclave are referred to as 'cat people' for their furtive darting between the shadows. Attracted to this other world are those who remember the intimacy of the mythical city. It is here that I have often met Masahisa Fukase.

Fukase came down to the city in the Fifties from the northern island of Hokkaido, where his father ran a photo studio in a small town. As a photography student, he habitually documented his life in the city. He has recently been re-examining many of these photographs. The place names of the pictures – Shinjuku or Ikebukuro – are the familiar landmarks, but the landscape of his photographs suggests not another decade, but another century. He recorded the old apartment houses, the children playing freely in the backstreets, the local gangster, the big American servicemen having their shoes shined, the street vendors, and the Shinjuku alleys lined with small bars at night. Yanaka, the Golden Gai, or the old photographs of Fukase constitute a world drawn out on a human scale, a world of intimate, domestic drama, where the rhythm of daily life continues, despite the transformations that are occurring out of view.

The single most important contribution to a changing photography in Japan was the arrival in Tokyo in 1957 of William Klein's book, *New York* (1956). With the bold subtitle *Trance Witness Revels* the book declared its tone with the voice of newspaper headlines. It shouted with unprecedented volume. 'I saw the book as a monster big city "Daily Bugle", with its scandals and scoops, that you'd find blowing in the streets at three

*Quotation from Wim Wenders's narration in *Tokyo-Ga*, 1984.

Masahisa Fukase: Ikebukuro, Tokyo, 1950s

Above Masahisa Fukase: Tokyo, 1950s
Following spread William Klein: Tatsumi Hijikata, Kata Miyazawa and Kazuo Ohno in
Improvising Dance Happening, Toyko, 1961

in the morning,' said Klein. 'I could imagine my pictures lying in the gutter like the New York "Daily News".'*

Klein had overturned photography, particularly the objective disciplines of Cartier-Bresson, which were dominant in Europe. He incorporated distortion, blur, wide-angle views and grain into his vocabulary and created a new dynamic. It was a great moment in the history of the medium, as rough and roaring as the first howling sounds of an amplified guitar. The book had a kinetic form in correspondence to the dynamic of the city. It was nearer to the spirit of music or the abstraction of painting than to photography. The pace was like that of film, creating a cumulative layering of imagery. Purity, reduction, and the art of simplification expressed in the metaphysics of American photography from Stieglitz to Weston had been displaced by a collage effect, by density and bold graphic strokes like those of a painter. Klein had photographed a world in flux; he had found the language of chaos. For astute Japanese, he offered a strategy with which they could encounter the layers of their own chaos. The strategy was contagious.

Klein's freedom was achieved from a point both outside New York and outside photography, with a stated mistrust of the photographic establishment. Following his demobilisation from the United States Army after the war, he moved to Paris to become a painter and he worked for several months at the studio of Fernand Léger, though he confesses that it was Léger's ideas rather than his painting that were most influential. Léger was challenging forms and searching for a new language for the industrial age. 'He wanted us to get out of the studios and into the streets, or link up with architects as he had with Le Corbusier. He wanted us to be *monumental*,' said Klein.* His own early paintings were large geometrical and typographical forms; he was incorporating language and escalating scale by working on large panels.

It was Alexander Liberman, the art director of *Vogue*, who saw Klein's work in Paris and realised its extraordinary potential. His support led to Klein's return to New York and to the eventual creation of the work for the *New York* book. After six years in Europe, Klein was distanced from the city in which he grew up and which he both loved and hated. 'I was in a trance. But I was able to do something about what I felt. I had a camera, though I barely knew how to use it.' Klein took on the city with ferocity as if he was settling old scores, 'I thought New York had it coming, that it needed a kick in the balls.'*

Liberman saw the dynamic in the New York work, 'This incredible flow beyond the actual frame, like moments from a film. In my experience, he was the first to bring into photography what Léger had achieved in art – the glorification of the life and rhythms of the street.'* The street was Klein's domain, and indeed his inevitable exploration of film began on one of the best-known streets in the world. His first film, *Broadway by Light*, made in 1958, was almost an extension to the cinematic drama of the *New York* book. Klein suggests that it might be the first film from the culture of Pop Art. He was of the same generation as the artist, Robert Rauschenberg, an instigator of that culture, who after his discharge from the Navy had also gone to Paris to study painting. While

*John Heilpern, 'Profile', *William Klein*, Aperture, New York, 1981.

Above William Klein: *Cinema poster*, Tokyo, 1961
Following spreads William Klein: *Outskirts of Tokyo and Sony Sign*, 1961; *Les Liaisons Dangereuses*, Tokyo, 1961;
Fresh Fruits, Tokyo, 1961.

駐
NO PARKING
東京都公安委員会
東京都公安委員会
ロードショウ
8より
ニュー東宝
ナチ残虐行為の全貌！
ストラスバーグ主演
イタリフィルム
提供

Klein was photographing on the streets of New York in 1954 and 1955, Rauschenberg had a studio in the same building as his friend, Jasper Johns, on Pearl Street. Rauschenberg was also turning to newspaper headlines and graffiti. 'New York is a maze of unorganised experiences peopled by the unexpected,' Rauschenberg later said.*

Klein returned to Paris to publish *New York*, sensing hostility within his native city. It was Chris Marker, the film-maker, then an editor with the French publishing house Editions du Seuil, who stated his commitment to the book. It was published as Number 1 in the series *Album Petite Planète*. Marker was an appropriate ally. Federico Fellini was among the admirers of *New York* and he invited Klein to Rome to work as an assistant. The streets of Rome provided Klein with further layers of history, language and graffiti. The vitality of the streets was also drawn from the processions of the devoutly Catholic inhabitants. Marker published *Rome* in 1959 as *Album Petite Planète*, Number 3.

By 1960 Klein had moved on at a furious pace; in addition to his photography in the fashion world and the development of his film work, he had begun to take photographs in Moscow, which was to become the subject for the third of his four-volume series on cities. Tokyo was his final destination and the book, *Tokyo* (1964), marked not only the end of the series, but also the displacement of his photography by his film-making. Like Robert Frank, after an intense period of redefining the possibilities of photography, the sequential effect of his work inevitably led him to explore the movement of film.

The response to Klein's *New York* had extended beyond the Japanese photography world, though it was inspirational to a number of critics and photographers. Tadanori Yokoo remembered the impact of the book in 1960 on the designers of the Nippon Design Centre, where he worked alongside Ikko Tanaka. Klein was invited to Japan by a Japanese editor and the subsequent book, *Tokyo*, deepened his impact on the Japanese. 'I must confess my attempts to steal Klein's sense and technique in order to obtain the same perspective as he had when he saw and expressed Tokyo,' wrote Yokoo.† The most creative figures in Japan were learning how to approach their native culture through the distanced perspective of a foreigner, who declared he knew nothing of their world.

'Aux Indes rien à voir, tout à interpréter, dit Henri Michaux. À Tokyo, je pensais: tout à voir, rien à interpréter, je serais le Barbare a Tokyo,' Klein stated in his introduction to *Tokyo*. He told me in a recent conversation that he had seen interesting new photographs by Japanese photographers at the time, and he thought that Japan would offer him a fresh vision. When he arrived there, all he saw were photographs that looked like his own. Such was the strength of his influence that Klein, 'the Barbarian', crossed from West to East, to find the distorted mirror image of his own work. Indeed, when the Japanese printers worked on *Tokyo*, they missed the mid-tone greys that Klein was exploring, and they printed the work in stark black and white contrast, in imitation of his earlier work. At all levels Klein's language was both absorbed and imitated.

While the circle of culture recycled Klein, the world he entered was as unfamiliar

*Robert Rauschenberg, statement for unreleased film: *Mostly About Rauschenberg* (produced by Reiner Moritz 1974–5). In Lawrence Alloway, 'Rauschenberg's Development', *Robert Rauschenberg*, Staatliche Kunsthalle, Berlin, 1980.

†*William Klein*, P.P.S., Tokyo, 1987.

as another planet, where he had no scores to settle and where he knew nothing of the language or social gestures. Besides the inherent qualities of a hieroglyphic sign language and the density of the Japanese city, the street offered Klein a purely detached graphic experience. Every action was ritualised. Whether he was in the gym, at the Kabuki theatre, on a street in the Ginza, or at a sports stadium, he was observing the flow of ceremony. The city itself became theatre.

At the beginning of *Tokyo*, opening with a section entitled *Ceremonies*, are Klein's photographs of Tatsumi Hijikata in a sequence with the dancer, Kazuo Ohno, performing a dance adaptation of Jean Genet's *Notre Dame des Fleurs* through a Tokyo back street. In one famous picture, Hijikata, his head in a black hood, appears to leap out at the camera. From that point on, all Klein's Tokyo photographs are pieces in an alien drama. The second section, *Album*, takes the viewer out on to the sidewalks and the trains, and into the great masses of the Tokyo population. The final section, *Ikebana*, named after Japanese flower arrangement, explores the sign language as pure calligraphic abstraction. In Tokyo Klein found a hieroglyphic maze, which reinforced all Léger's emphasis on a search for a public, monumental art. The art had already been written across the billboards of Japan. Towards the end of the book Klein presents a famous view, a point of entrance not exit, on the way into Tokyo from Haneda airport. It would have formed the first impression of the city for the arriving traveller. It was a wall of advertisements declaring WELCOME above a Sony sign, beside a congested canal which looks like a scene from Edo. This entrance, the outermost façade of the city, is as illusory as a film set.

Klein had direct contact with a number of Japanese photographers since he was using the dark-rooms of the VIVO group, a collective that had evolved out of the *Junin-no-me*, (The Eyes of Ten), the core of post-war photographic talent and which included Shomei Tomatsu and Eikoh Hosoe. Tomatsu had indeed produced a great body of work on the streets of Tokyo himself before his Shinjuku document. However, it was the younger generation, at a stage when they were most receptive, who were evidently affected by Klein.

Daido Moriyama, at one time Hosoe's assistant, had seen Klein's *New York*. 'I was so touched and provoked by Klein's photo book, that I spent all my time on the streets of Shinjuku mixing myself in with the noise and the crowds, doing nothing except clicking, with abandon, the shutter . . .'* Moriyama's work represents the breakthrough of the first post-Klein generation in Japan. In the Japanese assimilative style, he imitated, absorbed and finally 'Japanised' the lessons of Klein. Realising Klein's audacity, and his ability to use chaos as his substance and to incorporate the discarded fragments of imagery like the crumpled newspaper in the gutter, Moriyama turned to his native culture with all the predatory assertiveness he witnessed in Klein.

Moriyama's background was balanced between the anarchic tendencies of his wayward adolescence and tight, formal discipline. He had grown up in Osaka and as a teenager in the Fifties he spent much of his time wandering in the downtown streets of the entertainment area. He worked in a design studio but drifted in the bars and *pachinko* parlours. He

*William Klein, P.P.S., Tokyo, 1987.

Following spreads Masatoshi Naitoh: from *Tokyo 1970–1985*, 1985

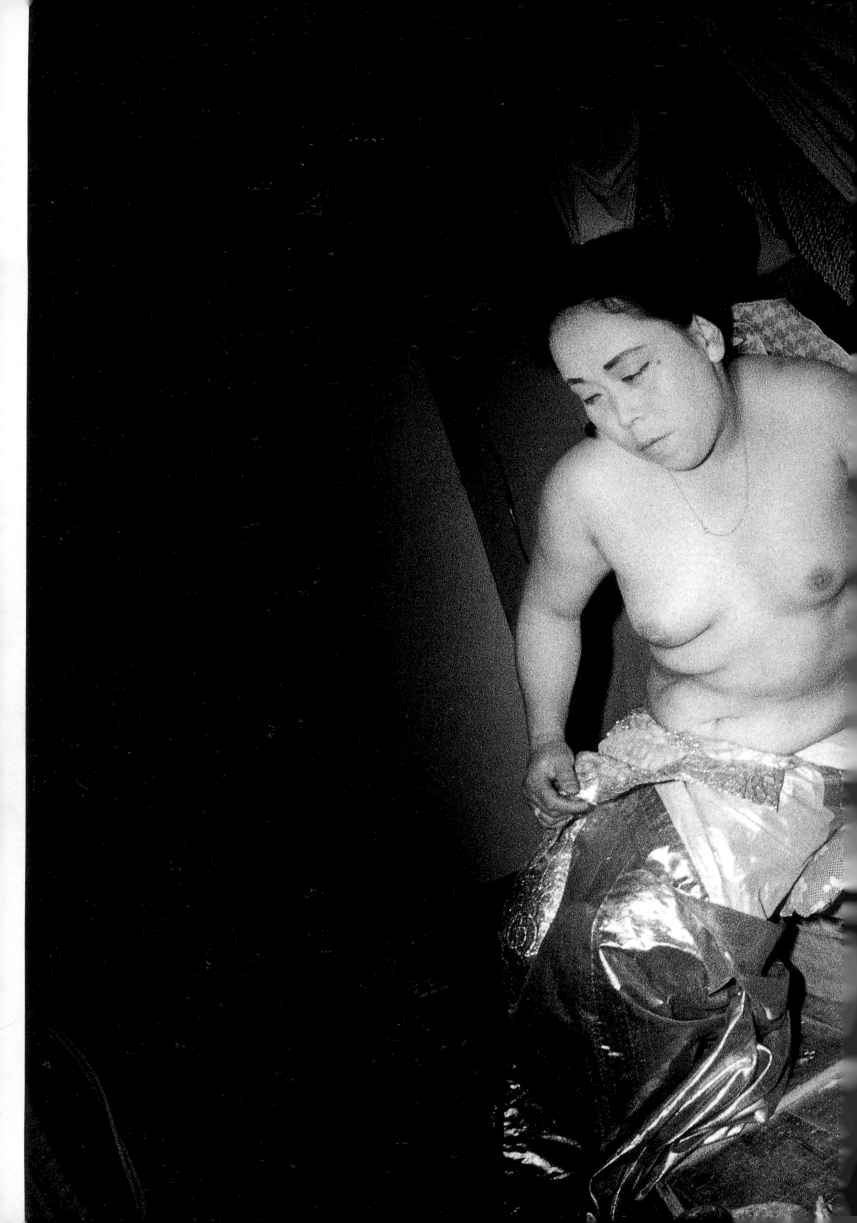

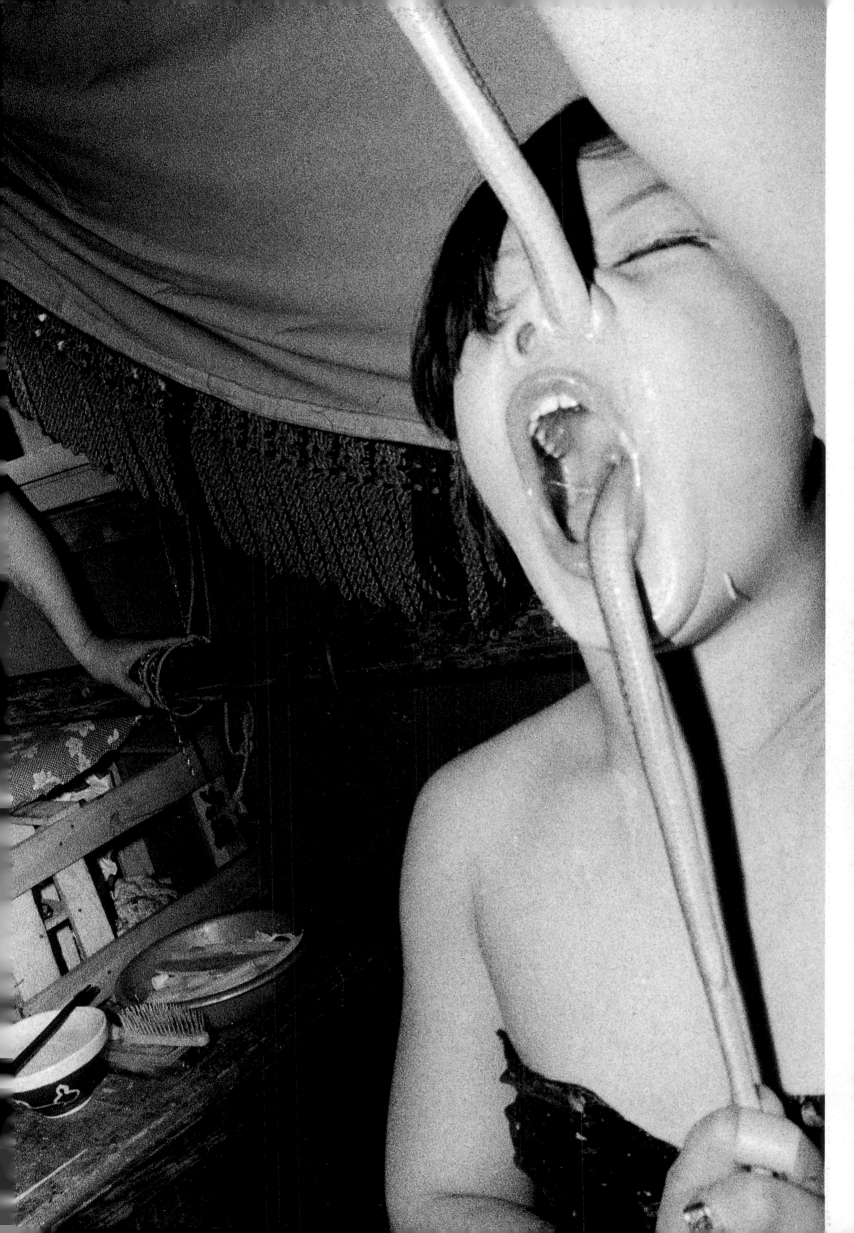

served an apprenticeship with the formal landscape photographer Takeji Iwamiya, but he moved to Tokyo with the hope of working for VIVO, since he greatly admired the work of Tomatsu. Hosoe took him on as his assistant, but recognising his talents, encouraged him to be independent.

Shuji Terayama had noticed some of Moriyama's photographs of rubbish and thought them to be beautiful. Moriyama remembers being approached by the writer who wanted Moriyama to illustrate some essays he was about to publish at that time in the late Sixties. Terayama appeared like a movie star not a writer and took Moriyama off into a new world of the underground theatre.

In the east of the city, beyond Yanaka and Ueno, is the district of Asakusa, a world of traders and merchants centred around the famous temple of Senso-ji. Far from the grandeur of the Ginza or the centres of Shinjuku or Shibuya, Asakusa is like a separate small town of shops and bars. It has an underworld and theatrical tradition. It was once a home to travelling entertainers and actors, and is again reminiscent of Carné's *Les Enfants du Paradis*, where elements of crime, eroticism and popular theatre are merged. After Terayama's introduction, Moriyama entered the mysterious, peripheral world and photographed it with a heightened predatory and voyeuristic sense. Much of this work was included in his first book, *Nippon Theatre* (1968), in which he broke all conventions of layout and sequence. The book took the viewer through the fragmented experience between the back streets of Japan, in all their graphic chaos, and the dark interiors of underground performers, strippers, dressing rooms and small stages. Moriyama was cutting between the interior of theatre and the world outside as though editing film.

The photographer as predator was subsequently defined by Moriyama in the title of a later book, *A Hunter* (1972), in which he prowled the alleys near the American bases. Not only were the back streets his terrain, with the suggestion of the scene of a crime like Atget's empty Paris streets, Moriyama seemed to stalk his patch like a criminal. By 1972 he had forced his work to an extreme in *Farewell to Photography* (1972), a subversive anti-book in which he disrupted not only sequence, but all formal composition. He photographed in a single day in which a range of human experience was played out – sex, trains, death, newspaper cuttings, sidewalks, buttocks, crowds, nostrils, supermarket shelves, long grass, the ocean, breasts – all abstracted by the camera, and ravaged and scratched by the developing and printing process. The pages of the book bleed continuously to their edges and frequently reproduce the sprocket marks of the film. It was as if Moriyama was fighting the conventions of the rectangular frame, the windows on the world, where photographs correspond to photography itself, not to experience. He wanted to use the camera to photograph in a way that was equivalent to the world he actually saw and the way he saw it – a blurred, ruptured world at the heart of the city.

He returned to the format of *Nippon Theatre*, ten years after its original publication, in *Japan, a Photo Theatre II* (1978), and turned his abstractions into astonishing, poetic chains of juxtapositions – the eye of a fish meeting the headlamp of a car, and all the textures and fabrics of the street melting into pure surfaces. The abstraction, far from nullifying the experience of the street, only intensified the sense of danger and excitement. At the very centre of Tokyo, in the middle of the great maze, Moriyama found language to describe what one might actually see, beneath the cables, the bombardment of the sign language, and in the density of humanity.

Out in the wastelands, on the edges of the city, Moriyama has gone on to find the rusting remnants of industrial machinery, abandoned factory yards, amidst weeds and rubble, discarded bottles, paint-spattered shoes and all the disconnected fragments of the landscape. They coincide with his memory of the smells and wanderings of his early years in Osaka in the aftermath of the war. Now, with his photographic facility, he conducts his transmutations, elevating the rubble, the scarred walls and the empty lots to luminous forms, as if he was writing in the hieroglyphs of his own invented language.

His influence over young Japanese photographers in the Seventies was great and he passed on the lessons of Klein. He showed that it was possible to go out into the streets and engage anybody or anything with the camera. He began to teach in the Seventies in his own informal workshop. Keizo Kitajima, who went on to New York and whose book *New York* (1982), was directly in the line of Klein and Moriyama, remembers attending Moriyama's classes. 'We talked a lot about photographic art, like that of William Klein and Atget. Mr Moriyama was very interested in these two photographers, but most of the time we just drank and played chess and sat around talking.'* In an interview with Kitajima, Akira Suei remembered meeting Moriyama and asking if he was discussing photography: 'I was surprised when he answered that he mostly talked about women and drank.'* Moriyama's stance soon attracted a following. Seiji Kurata, another of Moriyama's pupils, became a photographer as a direct result of seeing his work. Kurata then went into the Tokyo streets at night with a large Pentax 6 x 7 and a flash and entered the nocturnal underworld.

Through the work of Weegee and of Diane Arbus, street violence and freaks had entered photographic vocabulary. Kurata, like Weegee, followed the police and the world of gang fights, *yakuza*, motorcycle boys and motorcycle deaths. His book *Flash-Up* (1980), involved a descent into the separate clans of the Tokyo underworld. In the midst of one of the safest cities, in a society which is viewed as one of the most conformist, Kurata introduced the viewer to transvestites, tattooed gangsters, bar-girls, ultra-right nationalist fanatics, leather boys who look like they'd walked off the streets of East Harlem, glue-sniffers, and the late-train riders. Kurata's *Flash-Up*, as its title implies, exposed a face of Tokyo which was brutal, steamy and dangerous. Behind the social precision, the efficiency of the department stores, the cleanliness and frequency of the trains, and the barrage of the blazing city, were encounters as wild as those of 125th Street or as degrading as those of the Bowery.

Masatoshi Naitoh also photographed the Tokyo underworld, and especially the destitute, but found a mythical place, resonant of Edo, that lurked in the darkest corners of the city. Naitoh also prowled the streets at night among the wounded, the arrested, the all-night girls, the entertainers and the homeless. Naitoh's imagery is not of violence but of darkness. 'In this megalopolis we call "Tokyo" I sometimes find here and there dark crater-like spots. Right below some neon sign there may be a certain darkness

*Keizo Kitajima, *New York*, Tokyo, 1982.

Following spreads Daido Moriyama: *Eyes (Viewpoint from the City)*, Aomori City, from *Lettre à St. Lou*, 1990; *Doorhandle*, from *Hikari to Kage (Light and Shadow)*, 1982; *Poster (Frustrated Female Bodies)*; *Aloha (As Worn by Young Gangsters)*, from *Japan; A Photo Theatre II*, 1978; *Cabbage (Decaying Plant)*; *Engine (Guts of Civilization)* from *Hikari to Kage (Light and Shadow)*, 1982; *Residential Area (Deserted Townscape)*; *Tights (The World of Mesh)*, Tokyo, from *Lettre à St. Lou*, 1990; *Man (Yawning in the Afternoon)*.

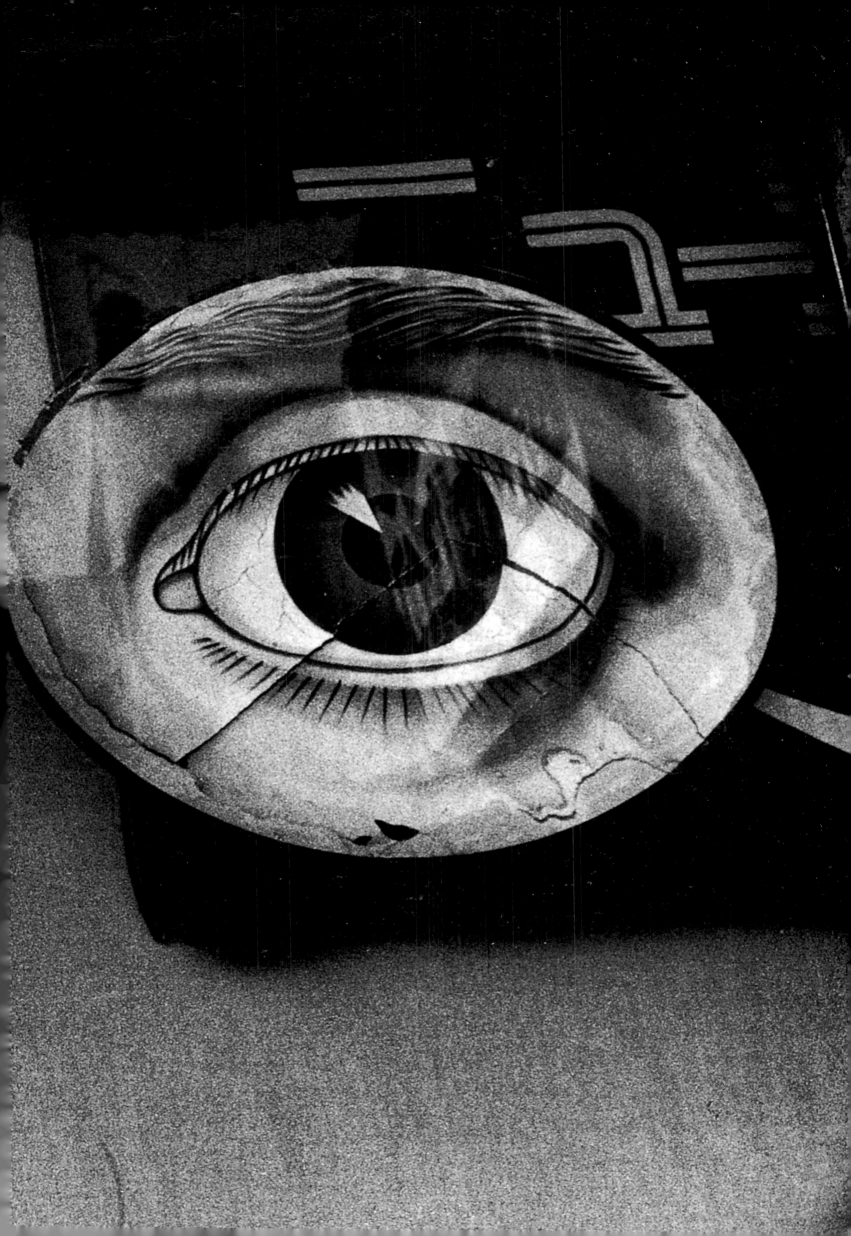

熟れた女の淫らなうめき！
☆これが問題の"プライベー
ポルノ"!!
★全世界大ヒット！遂にやってきた《未亡人》シリーズ第一弾！
監督 バート・トランバリー
音楽 ポール・ベルマン
オルガ・クリス
エマニエル・レッツ
カリーヌ・ステファン
HOT WIDOWS
《カラー作品》成人映画
映倫

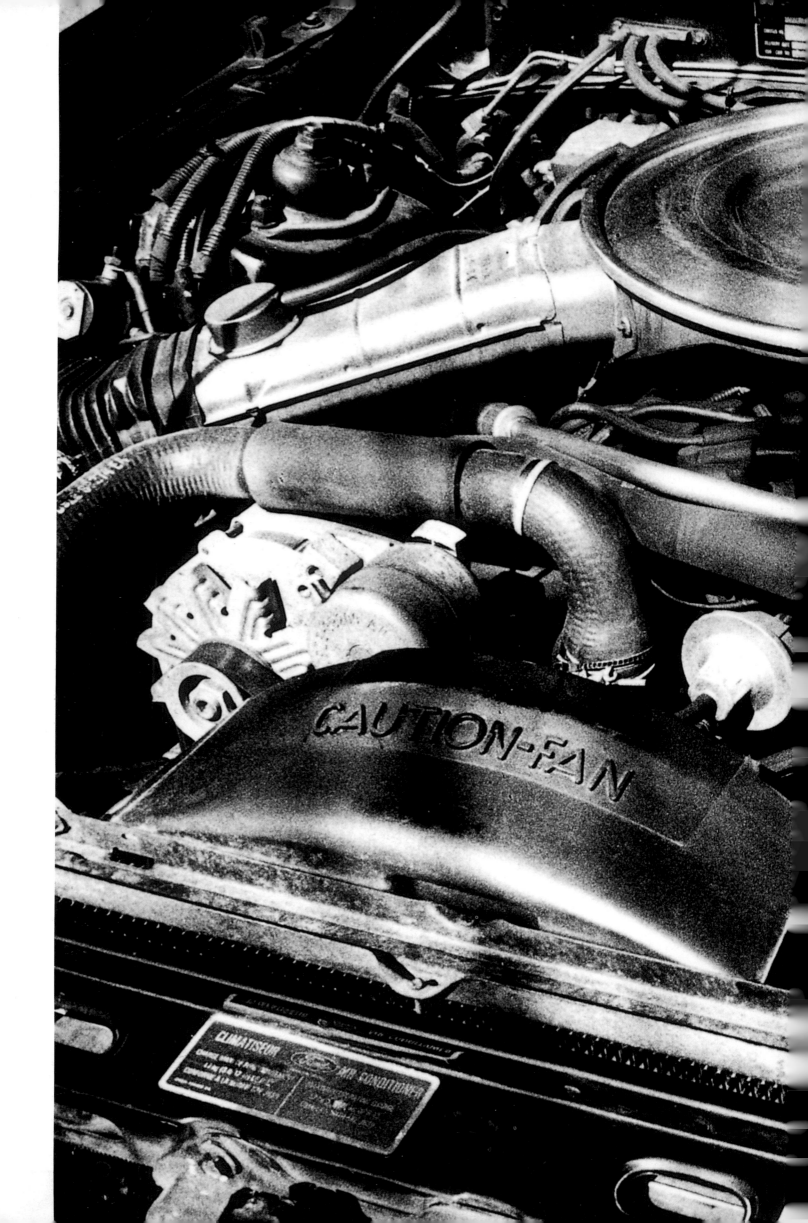

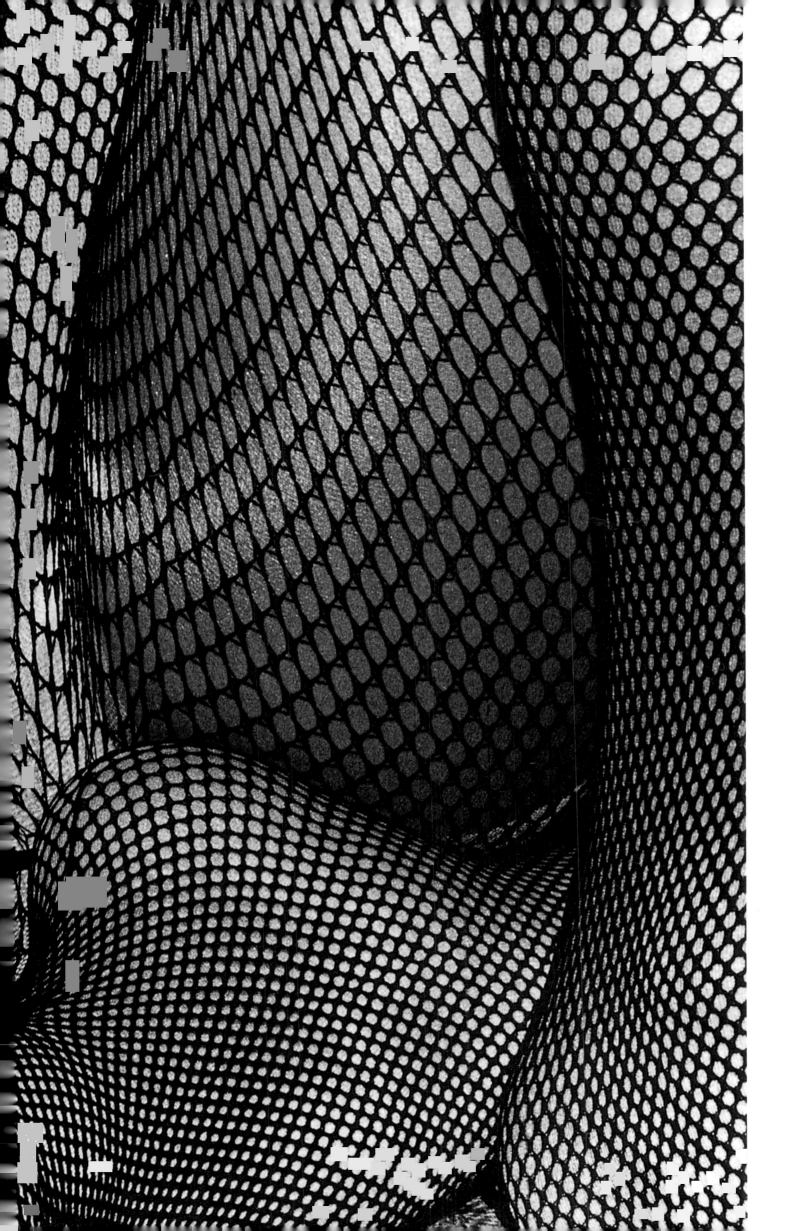

that makes me think of the mysteries of the black hole. Perhaps it is there, in that obscurity and mystery, that the real psyche of Tokyo is hidden and can be discerned.'*

Naitoh was digging like an archaeologist beneath the layers of the city to find the ghosts of Edo, the remnants of the foundations of the city. In the introduction to *Tokyo* (1985), Naitoh pointed out that four centuries ago, the site of Tokyo was a wilderness that grew into Edo, the largest city in the world, in the space of a single century. The city foundations were connected to traditions of magic with the founding of the Imperial Palace as the central axis, from which the city radiated out according to geomantic tradition. In his search for archaic evidence he found a cast of demonic characters, witches and guardians of this other world. 'Edo, a darkness that yet shines, continues to reveal the depths of the mind, nurturing itself still in such Kabuki plays as "The Ghosts of Yotsuya",' claimed Naitoh.*

Initially, like Terayama and Moriyama, Naitoh was drawn to the theatre groups in Asakusa. He joined *Komasa Ichiza*, a group of travelling players with such names as Oppai san and the Mermaid. They travelled from Asakusa all over Japan, performing like a small circus. Oppai san could swallow nails and live chickens or pass snakes through her nostrils. They were the last of an old Edo popular theatrical tradition, which had existed side by side with a changing city until the mid-Seventies when the Inamura Genkijo Theatre in Asakusa was destroyed. Naitoh's photographs were used as posters and hung from their tent. His exploration of this Asakusa culture led him to the gangster world of the *yakuza*. He decided to connect all his fragments and to reconstitute them as elements of his mythical Tokyo.

Naitoh was an anthropologist before he was a photographer. His first exhibition came from his study of mummies in the Tohoku district of northern Japan. One of his early books, *Baba* (1979) was drawn from his photographs of the *itako*, the women spirit mediums of the far north. They had access to another world and participated in trances and magic. Naitoh not only observed this world, but began to participate within it. He became a *yamabushi*, a spirit technician or shaman, after rigorous initiation in the Yamagata mountains, and has now acquired the shamanistic name, *Kenshuin*.

The dancer Hijikata referred to his own form of *Butoh* as *Ankoku Butoh*, implying a black theatre. Hijikata grew up in the far north of Tohoku amidst the same shamanistic traditions and contacts with the spirit world. Like Naitoh, Hijikata often referred to darkness as a source of the imagination. Naitoh now talks of a loss of darkness and his work has been published with an emphatically dark aesthetic. The luminous, electric city is a challenge to his archaic shadow land. More than fifty years ago Junichiro Tanizaki had defined darkness as residual in the Japanese imagination in his essay *In Praise of Shadows*. Naitoh finds a true Japan in the contradictory roles of a *yamabushi* in the mountains of the far north and as an inhabitant of the sprawling megalopolis of the future. In Tokyo he stalks the darkest alleys where the shadow world is preserved and which the blazing lights can never reach.

In Tokyo you can encounter your mirror image, Japanised and distorted. You can

*Masatoshi Naitoh, *Tokyo*, Meicho Publishing, Tokyo, 1985.

Above Kikuji Kawada: *Kiss on a Wall*, Shibuya, Tokyo, 1978, from *Los Caprichos*
Following spreads Kikuji Kawada: *Movie Star in a Car*, Mita, Tokyo, 1972; *Space Square*, Toyosu, Tokyo, 1978.
Both from *Los Caprichos*.

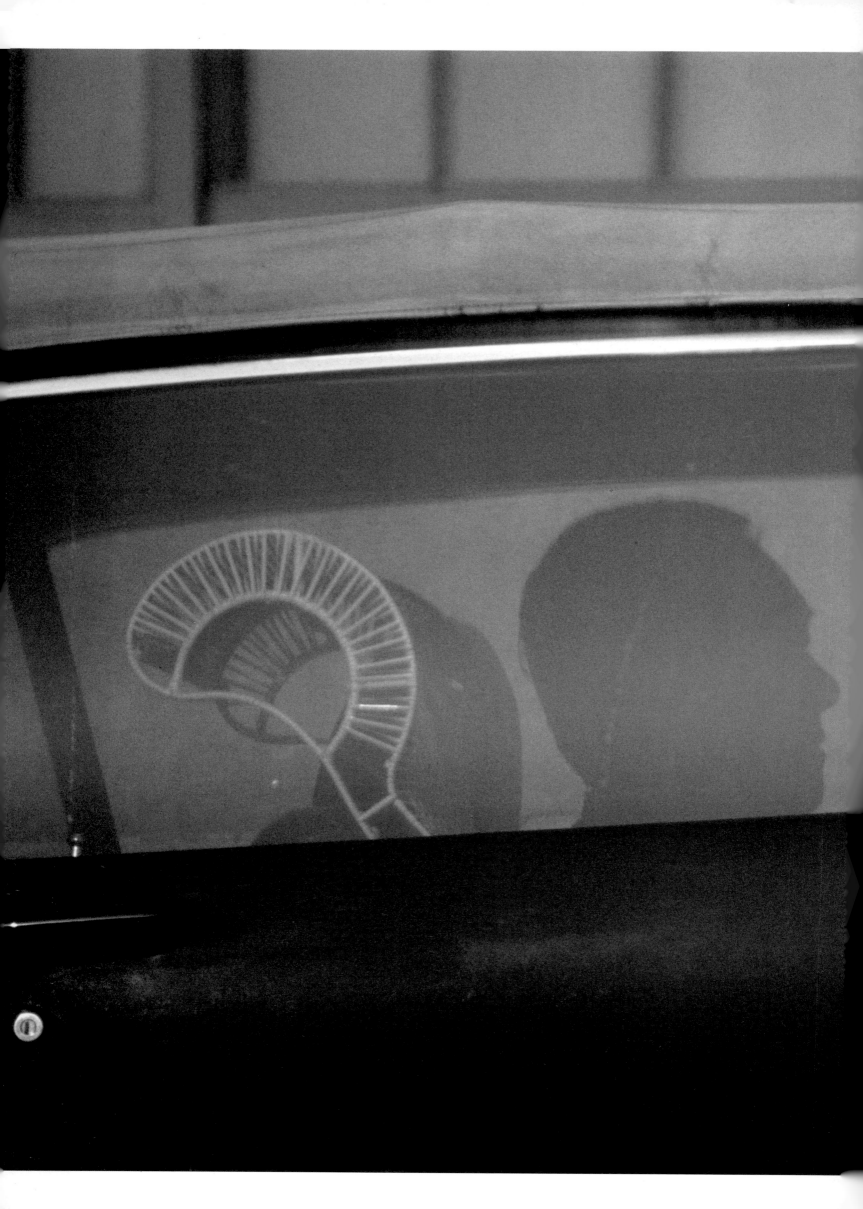

David Byrne: *Neighbourhood Map and Coke Machine*, Tokyo, from *Parkett*, 23, 1990

David Byrne: Tokyo, 1986

David Byrne: *Real Estate Office*, Roppongi, Tokyo, from *Parkett* 23, 1990

Above David Byrne: Tckyo, 1986
Following spread David Byrne: *Vending Machines on the Street Corner*, Tokyo, from *Parkett* 23, 1990

queue up to see Van Gogh's *Sunflowers*, buy English hunting breeches or hear Wagner between the pop records from the giant video screen across the square. Tokyo, so hard to define, a place beyond categories, deals frequently in clichés, even its own clichés. Now there is a challenge to find imagery that transcends the cliché yet truly resounds with the encounters of the street like the view of traffic, lights, signs, the hair on a woman's shoulder, the back of a man's shirt or crushed fruit on the ground.

Kawada, who had photographed *Chizu* (*The Map*), in the blackest abstraction, photographed the Tokyo streets throughout the Seventies in colour which seemed shocking. He called the series *Los Caprichos* after Goya. It reflects the most detached view of the city, the greatest alienation. He photographed crowds wandering in Space Square surrounded by murals of spacecraft. He focused on the suits of astronauts, a blazing car, the X-ray of a madman's head, a transistor circuit, and a human kiss painted in flesh tones on the concrete blocks of a wall in Shibuya as evidence of the human street. More recently, David Byrne, musician and film-maker, spent time photographing Tokyo. He had looked closely at the prolific output of the American colour photographer, William Eggleston, who was an expert on points of profound chaos. Byrne suggested there was a pattern, 'There are no aesthetic accidents . . . even the seeming chaos on the streets is intentional . . . the resulting complaints and criticisms of our urban environment are, in turn, also part of the environment. The occasional rupture is part of the texture.'*

Sometimes, after weeks of no contact with the outside, I have walked to the densest intersection of the city and felt invisible. A huge crowd, whose language I do not speak, whose body gestures I do not fully understand, walks past me, envelops me, and shows no sign of recognition. That point is the axis, the centre of the map. Theories of Japan are displaced by the sheer momentum of experience. The borrowed imagery of film and photographs is discarded as if I had actually entered a film and was participating on the screen I was witnessing. There are no resources left but pure observation. The city, with all its raging signals displayed around me, is an abstract wall. I engage with the inhabitants as through a filter; they hardly see me. I walk on down the street and track my progress a chain of steps, or a sentence in a new visual language.

*David Byrne, *Parkett 23*, Zurich, 1990.

Masahisa Fukase: *Posterity of Himiko*, performance in a helicopter over the Diet Building, Tokyo, 1971

5

BEYOND JAPAN

THE ENTRANCE TO the Miyake Design Studio is up the steps of a grey, concrete building, as solid as a fortress, in a quiet, elegant neighbourhood, not far from Shibuya. Walking from the nearby station I noticed a Sèvres shop window in which the china is arranged in high kitsch style. Fine china, velvet and brocade are the acquired trappings of Japanese wealth. European culture seems to be perceived as a television commercial parody of Versailles. The concrete of the Miyake Design Studio is a modern defence against the vulgarity of such trappings, as it is against the exterior chaos and contradictions of the city.

I pass a newly installed late Noguchi sculpture of balanced male and female form in the courtyard. On entering the building, Issey's eye is immediately evident. African tribal art and Irving Penn platinum prints of cigarette butts form the extreme conjunctions of visual invention and quality of execution on modern walls as textured as the earth in an African hut. The Miyake Design Studio, Issey's workplace and the centre of a large business, is clearly at a creative intersection, which is neither East nor West, but where the flamboyance of the 'primitive' meets modern refinement. The cigarette butts printed in platinum are, of course, distinguished examples of photographic alchemy. In Penn's photography Issey has found the work of an ally, whose eye is as reductive as his own – an eye that makes order out of chaos or sublime elegance out of dirt.

Before coming to the studio I had been advised by Issey's staff to visit an exhibition of the pots of Lucy Rie which Issey had organised. He had seen her work in a book in London and had sought her out. Now in her eighties, she has lived in London for more than fifty years since fleeing the Nazis in Vienna. Issey found in her work a lightness that was quite absent in the Japanese tea bowl, by now so weighted with historical and spiritual association. He recognised a sense of immediacy and simplicity. It was close to a 'Japanese' sensibility in its purest form, uncluttered by history. At the same time it was completely un-Japanese; it was the work of a Viennese refugee who had never been to Japan and whose style was distinct from the English potter, Bernard Leach, who had learned so much from the Japanese ceramic tradition.

The Sogetsu Kaikan, where Issey had arranged the exhibition, is a Kenzo Tange building in the centre of Tokyo with a huge entrance lobby designed by Noguchi. It is the corporate headquarters of a school of *ikebana*, flower arrangement. The installation was executed by Tadao Ando, the celebrated architect from Osaka. Several pots were placed on low plinths at the end of an enormous table surface covered with small stones like the gravel of a dry sand garden. At first glance they appeared to be resting on glass above the stones, but touching the surface I found it was water. It was an elemental arrangement with light on water above a surface which echoed the sand of a beach.

Issey is a great producer and his enthusiasm was creating a new cultural route. He wanted next to take the installation to England, which seemed to fulfil a circular pattern. Lucy Rie's work, in contrast to the decorative excesses of Viennese tradition, had been recognised for its purity and directness in Japan and had been exhibited in an institution dedicated to a traditional Japanese aesthetic. To return the work to its starting point in Britain marked the full circle of international culture.

Issey as a producer, chooses his cast carefully. Even the choice of a photographer for the Lucy Rie catalogue was highly calculated. Yasuhiro Ishimoto, whom Issey invited to photograph the pots had extensively photographed the Katsura Palace, the seventeenth-century masterpiece of Japanese architecture which had so influenced Western modern design. Ishimoto himself was almost bicultural, since he had studied photography in Chicago where the Institute of Design had been established as a new Bauhaus. He was a photographer who had gone outside Japanese tradition, yet returned from Chicago to Katsura, which in turn was another circular cultural route.

Tadao Ando, who installed the exhibition, is an architect with a brilliant reputation in both America and Japan. He is also unorthodox since he had been a boxer and is self-taught as an architect. Water had conspicuously featured in his design of a church, which a client has now built on the northern island of Hokkaido. His buildings also include a tea-house, the most refined Japanese architectural space, which he has built with both concrete walls and *tatami* mats on the ground. He has even built a vast, mobile circular theatre for the experimental group *Juro Kara*, based on a traditional theatre he had seen in Shikoku.

Ando clearly understands that tradition and innovation are not mutually exclusive forces. It is this central creative fact that links him to a great designer like Issey Miyake. It is that understanding that connects Ando to the very problems of modernism with which architects were struggling early in the century and that brings Ando full circle back to those problems at the end of the century. It was the understanding that innovation can reinforce tradition, which was exemplified by Stieglitz in the development of photography at the beginning of the century. Those traditions are both local and specific like the use of *tatami* mats, and universal like the aspiration of a Stieglitz 'equivalent' or the ideals of the modern movement in architecture.

Ando was invited to teach at Yale in 1987 and he described his intentions at the time in his essay *Learning from the Modern Movement*:

We are finally coming to an end of a period of worldwide pandemonium in architecture that began in the latter half of the 1960s. During this period of chaos, which has substantial significance as an antithesis in the modern movement, the postmodern sensibility instantly caught on internationally as a trend that began to create an atmosphere in which the sincere pursuit of genuine architectural concern was out of fashion and in which architects were allowed to create rules for their own pleasure.*

Ando was doing nothing less than attack the indulgences of post-modernism, challenging its licence, while accepting the inevitable healthy reaction of its revolt. He was emphasising again a resistance to chaos.

Noguchi recurs as a ghost in this process. Noguchi had exhibited his work on water in an exhibition in 1950 in Tokyo where, at that time, he was regarded as too 'Japanese' in his style, as later he would be regarded as too American. In the immediate post-war years Americanisation was dominant with such exhibitions as *Amerika seikatsu bunka ten* (Modern American Life) in Tokyo in 1947. For economic reasons Japanese designers were employing their skills to serve the massive forces of the Occupation. After years of insularity the Japanese were also outward looking and importing the work of American painters or Western photographers from Franz Kline to Henri Cartier-Bresson, Bill Brandt and Eugene Smith. Meanwhile Noguchi was seen to reassert native Japanese qualities. Whatever the circuitous route of his creativity or whatever his distance from Japan, he understood the fundamental principles of Japanese aesthetics, and the relationship of Japanese architecture to the elements. His understanding of this tradition may indeed have been acquired as a result of his actual distance from Japan, which allowed him to be more 'Japanese' than the Japanese themselves.

Like Noguchi, Ando redirects our sensibility to fundamental roots, both to the purity of Japanese tradition and the ideals of the modern movement in architecture. The two separate traditions, Eastern and Western, are mutually sympathetic and synthesised in his work. Noguchi is neither Japanese, nor American, but ultimately emphatically asserts both Eastern and Western tradition. Ando's desire for an uncluttered architectural purity, or Noguchi's desire for undecorated sculptural form, exists like Issey behind the concrete walls of his studio, in a Japan ravaged by the excesses of a post-modernist playground or a 'Bladerunner' culture after the film sets of Ridley Scott.

Japan has such momentum that chaos is an integral part of the landscape. As William Klein, the outsider, could adopt chaos as the graphic substance of his photography, foreign architects can freely indulge in their fantastic elements in the Japanese city with a liberty that would be unlikely in their native landscape. Nigel Coates, the English architect, has built a restaurant on Hokkaido modelled on Noah's Ark. Michael Graves is building a high-rise tower in Yokohama, that is described as looking like a robot.† This boom time for international architects caused Deyan Sudjic to comment:

*Tadao Ando, *The Yale Studio and Current Works*, Rizzoli, New York, 1989.

†Deyan Sudjic, 'Japan's hothouse flowers are built to wilt', *Sunday Correspondent*, 10 December 1989.

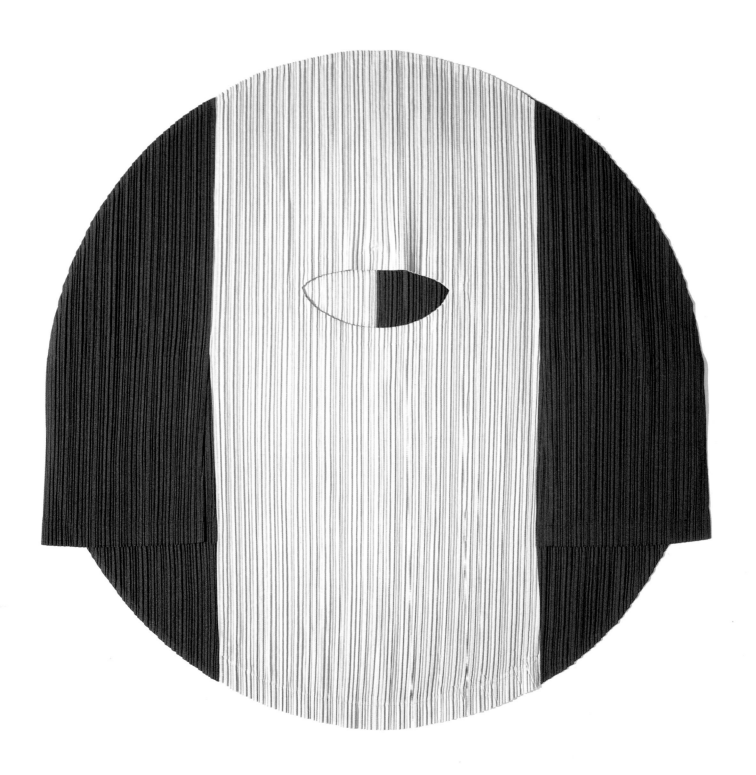

Irving Penn: Issey Miyake *Pleats*, 1990

The very fact that they are all building in Japan at the same time is enough to unite them in a movement that is neither modern nor post-modern, neither regionalist nor internationalist, but instead amounts to a hallucinatory fragment of a world, conceived by the circus of the perpetually jet-lagged, and put through the image blender that is modern Japan.*

Twenty years after William Klein produced his book *Tokyo* (1964), Chris Marker, who had been the editor of Klein's first book, produced a film masterpiece, *Sans Soleil* (1982), at the centre of which was Tokyo. The film moved geographically from Iceland to the Cape Verde Islands and repeatedly back to Japan. It was an account of a contemporary explorer who discovers Japan as if he was discovering a new planet, which remains as elusive or fictional as Planet Mongo. Marker not only shifts place, but shifts time. He fluctuates between the details of Sei Shonagon, writing in the tenth-century Heian court and a synthetic world existing within a television monitor. In the early Eighties the film seemed prophetic; through Japan, Marker was encountering the world. The result was layers of film and language as complicated as the global currents of information that constitute the density of the modern city:

Tokyo is a city criss-crossed by trains, tied together with electric wire, she shows her veins.

[Or] He told me that this city ought to be deciphered like a musical score. One could get lost in the great architectural masses and the accumulation of details, and that created the cheapest images of Tokyo: overcrowded, megalomaniacal, inhuman. He thought he saw more subtle cycles there, rhythms, clusters of faces caught sight of in passing, as different and precise as groups of instruments.

This exterior Japan is witnessed so intensely from a foreign position, by the detached observer. For the inhabitants who are still conscious of the chaos, or of the complexity of the imagery or the collisions of history, there is the creation of interior space or interior harmony as a means of survival. The fictional Japan that we as witnesses observe is invisible for those who inhabit the space, those who sleep on commuter trains, or effortlessly ride the subways, or shop at the busiest intersections. For them, it is not some *other* place, but the ground on which they walk.

Inside Issey's studio, within his ordered space, I sat at a bare table across from two of his staff, at the first of several meetings over a period of many months. With all the grace that is customary in such circumstances, when I started to describe my intention to create an exhibition or series of installations, which I called a 'Phototheatre', they thought I had come to work on another 'Japanese' exhibition.

His assistant turned to me and stated emphatically, as if to end the discussion, 'But Issey Miyake is not a Japanese designer.'

---

*Deyan Sudjic, 'Japan's hothouse flowers are built to wilt', *Sunday Correspondent*, 10 December 1989.

162

Irving Penn: Issey Miyake *Pleats*, 1990

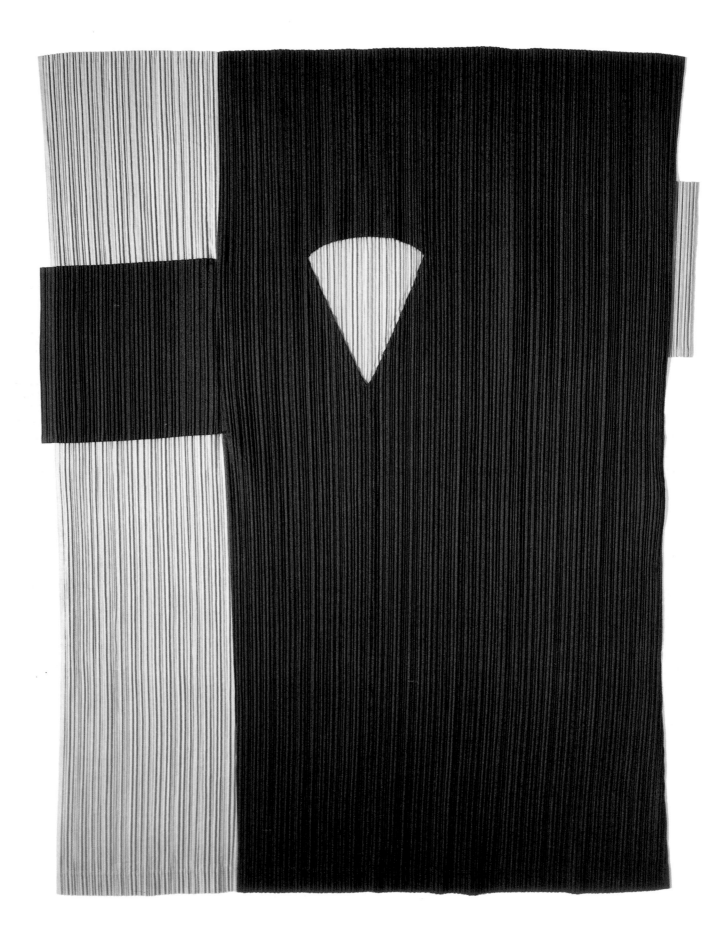

Irving Penn: Issey Miyake *Pleats*, 1990

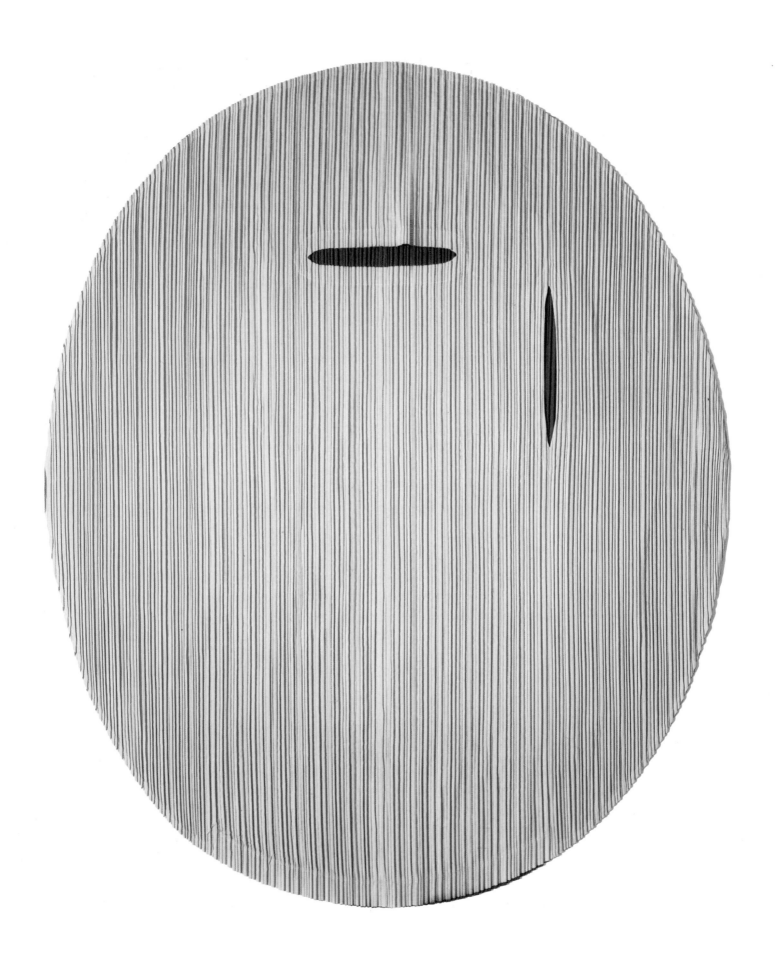

Irving Penn: Issey Miyake *Pleats*, 1990

This conversation occurred late in 1988 just after the book, *Issey Miyake: Photographs by Irving Penn*, had been published. The book stated the fact that Issey was born in Hiroshima in 1938, and that he had been 3.5 kilometres from the epicentre of the Hiroshima explosion. It was not a fact on which he chose to dwell. The circumstances of his upbringing would suggest that he had experienced modern Japanese history as directly as anyone of his generation. He resisted the implicit homogeneity of 'Japanese' designer as a category. It was as false as a school of 'Japanese' photography, which no more existed as a tangible entity than 'British' photography. To describe Ando as a 'Japanese' architect would represent a serious reduction in the identity of a man who had taught at both Yale and Columbia and whose achievements were celebrated internationally.

'My generation in Japan lived in limbo. We were the first really raised with Hollywood movies and Hershey bars, the first who had to look in another direction for a new identity. We dreamed between two worlds,' wrote Issey at this time.*

The resolution of the two worlds was a circular pattern. In Issey's book *Bodyworks* (1983), Andy Warhol was quoted with a complex remark about 'Man's . . . nebulous circumnavigation', which ended simply, 'East meets West and I like that because I've always liked circles more than squares. I like to watch people going around in circles.' Issey is attracted to both African and Indian textiles; he found Africa a great source of inspiration. 'Did you know there is a tree in Africa where the bark comes off completely?' he asked. 'It's round, just like a tube of jersey. I wanted to make something woven that was warped like African bark.'* So the circular, organic form was absorbed into his design. The architect Arata Isozaki, writing in Issey's *East Meets West* (1978), described the 'hollow loom', the *utsuhata*, on which were woven the seamless Japanese sacred garments for the gods – the prototype of clothing, which was a universal, seamless, circular form.

Issey's collaboration with Penn has taken the reductive principle to extremes. Penn photographed the clothes in white emptiness, and the images appeared flattened or abstracted in their isolation. The inspiration of organic forms was clear; there are echoes of shells, seaweed or the cocoons of insects in his designs. Issey guides the eye with a series of poetic equations. There are suggestions of water and sea. After collaborating further on Issey Miyake catalogues for 1989 and 1990, Penn photographed Issey's ultimate abstraction, his pleats. These were first shown at the Stedelijk Museum, Amsterdam in the exhibition, *Energies*, in April 1990, then in *Pleats Please* at the Touko Museum of Contemporary Art, Tokyo in September 1990. At both sites the dresses were placed flat at ground level in pure, geometric forms of circles, rectangles and ovals. Penn's photographs still further abstracted Issey's designs by removing all sense of scale, so equating them not with cloth but with minimalist painting.

In the catalogue to the Tokyo exhibition Toshiharu Ito described the fluidity of Issey's work, as if the period of binary fusion between East and West had been replaced by a new territory. That fluidity suggested a stage beyond any fixed equilibrium or convenient concept of cultural balance. Issey's working process was also described as being like that of a dancer. He designs not by sketching, but by wrapping cloth around the body. 'The clothes

Issey Miyake: Photographs by Irving Penn, New York Graphic Society, Little Brown, Boston, 1988.

Opposite Tadanori Yokoo: *The Barrier Has Been Broken Down*, silkscreen and paint, 1990 (170 × 115cm)

are born in the motion of my hands and body,' said Issey. In conclusion, Ito compared Issey's work to that of a shaman. Indeed, the work abounds with archaic connotation as he descends into a primary language. At the same time, he is the architect of a new medium, that transcends both the fashion world and fundamental cultural divisions – a vital position in the last decade of the century.

For many years Issey has worked with Tadanori Yokoo, whom he describes as 'the Utamaro of our time'. In the past Yokoo's designs have been used for textile prints by Issey. Yokoo continues to produce graphic designs for the Miyake Design Studio. Yokoo is of the same generation as Issey, though he was famous in Japan as a poster designer when Issey was still in Paris. He absorbed influences from outside Japan and travelled widely. He went to America, where his work was exhibited at the Museum of Modern Art in New York, and to India, where he was greatly inspired by Tantra Art, which entered his graphic vocabulary as did elements of the prevalent psychedelia of the times. Yokoo absorbed styles rapidly and married them to his own sense of a contemporary *ukiyo-e* design. In the late Sixties he enjoyed a celebrity status and was prominent in the underground as a founder member of *Tenjosajiki* and an associate of Terayama. As an actor, he starred in Oshima's film *Diary of a Shinjuku Thief* (1968). He was a friend of Hijikata and Hosoe, as well as a close collaborator with Mishima, who influenced him enormously.

Behind his prolific output and absorption of a wide variety of influences was a restlessness which came to a climax in his renunciation of his role as a designer and his desire to be a painter. In retrospect looking at his painting and drawing from the early Eighties, the influences of Jasper Johns, David Hockney or of the great wave of German expressionist painting, clearly could be stated. To the outsider, looking across the world to any available evidence of Yokoo's work, his identity which had been so defined as a great poster designer, was submerged by the disparity of the work. It was as if with his technical virtuosity he could parody the styles of Western art. Sometimes, looking through his catalogues one could feel the absorption and recycling of art as if by an alien intelligence. In making his decisive move to escape his role as a graphic designer, he was absorbing as much as was possible from the outside world in order to find his own language. It was evidently an essential, transitory period, but there was also a sense of isolation, which may be unfounded, of a man looking at the art world from a distance, wherever it revolved, as if through a great telescope. The isolation may have existed within Japan as much as between Yokoo's studio and the world beyond Japan. Throughout the Eighties he continued to work furiously and travel extensively.

His ingenuity led him to continue experimenting with a variety of media. He applied his graphic skills to the video with Lisa Lyon. He developed a technique using ceramic tiles with which he created a series of seven epic panels depicting the growth of Tokyo from the Edo period to the year 1986, when they were exhibited at the 'Tokyo: Form and Spirit' exhibition in Minneapolis in installations designed by Isozaki. The panels combined a collage-like superimposition of imagery in poster style with a sense of monumental rather than ephemeral art. Photography, film, *ukiyo-e* design, and painting were the elements in this iconography of historical transformation.

Yokoo's relationship with the West remained unclear since this work was evidently

Opposite Tadanori Yokoo; *We Are Patiently Awaiting You*, silkscreen and paint, 1990 (170 × 115cm)

Tadanori Yokoo: *Split Reality*, silkscreen and paint, 1990 (170 × 115cm)

Tadanori Yokoo: *Gates of Death*, silkscreen and paint, 1990 (170 × 115cm)

contemporary Japanese art, yet he continued to look for sources outside Japan, just as he needed to address not only his domestic patrons or supporters, but an international art world. Yokoo is approaching the Nineties by going back to the fundamental sources of Western painting. From our first meeting, he welcomed the opportunity to be placed *beyond* Japan.

Throughout 1990 he worked on a series of twenty pieces using silkscreen and paint, each about six feet high and four feet wide. The drama of the pieces is established by landscapes built up from sections of the human body. These are painted close-ups, as if through a camera lens, derived from Caravaggio, Delacroix, Titian and Velázquez. Limbs and folds of flesh, the corner of a Deposition, become hills and valleys. In the midst of this terrain are scenes from Hollywood cinema and obscure science-fiction movies. Details from Fritz Lang's *Metropolis* or the plane chase from Hitchcock's *North by North West* meet a Jasper Johns target. Occasionally on top of this drama is added the lined silhouette of a *ukiyo-e kabuki* actor, the ghost of a native tradition. This is the world to which Issey referred when he said that they came from a generation that dreamed in two worlds.

In 1887, three years before his death, Van Gogh took his *Japonisme* to an extreme by painting a *kabuki* actor, surrounded by Oriental motifs of bamboo, lotus flowers, and cranes, as if he had borrowed Utamaro quite literally. The same actor's wig and combs are there in Yokoo's silhouette in the new series. A hundred years after Van Gogh, Yokoo has reversed the process and pointed the telescope back at the tradition of Western art, which he has lifted, cropped and reinvented, collaging the fragments of his dreams, the details of half-remembered movies, with all his graphic brilliance.

Both Issey and Yokoo have passed from the realm of pure commerce. They clearly established themselves as artists by transcending the fashion and design industries. As a student Issey had attacked the establishment for failing to recognise the artistic legitimacy of fashion design. Issey no longer has to prove his status as an artist and Yokoo as a painter, but their backgrounds reveal their rise through the world of commercial enterprise, in synchronism with the great economic revival of post-war Japan. Significantly, the diverse creative figures of their generation who have affected the cultural climate both within and beyond Japan have emerged not from what Western tradition describes as 'fine art' but from the disciplines of applied arts, cinema and photography. Architects, graphic designers, fashion designers, art directors, and film directors, working with photographers and dancers, are interconnected. They, as much as industrialists or bankers, have created the map of contemporary Japan. They have also conspicuously demonstrated their work beyond Japan.

Photographic art in Japan, after the breakthroughs of the Sixties and Seventies, has been eclipsed by the flamboyance and inventiveness of advertising, video, and television. The fine photographic print has almost become an example of an arcane tradition, as it once was when Stieglitz was establishing his galleries in New York, or Frederick Sommer discovering alchemical symbols in the Arizona desert. Photography, the great popular medium, has come full circle with the century. Only now at the start of the Nineties has a Tokyo Metropolitan Museum of Photography been established, in the capital of the camera industry.

It was not until 1989–90 that Japanese art of the Eighties reached America in the exhibition *Against Nature*. When it arrived, it was no longer recognisable as 'Japanese'. Its title challenged any tradition of natural aesthetics. It looked like art. It could have been created in San Paolo or Zurich. Now, a new generation of artists has emerged who will be supported by the commerce of the gallery and the museum, not the commerce of industry. Outstanding figures like Shinro Ohtake are full of borrowed echoes like the ghost of Rauschenberg. In a post-modernist style Yasumasa Norimura takes on art history with himself as model, just like Cindy Sherman. Photography, as in the West, becomes marginalised to the periphery of the art world. But just as Ando describes a return in architecture to the problems and ideals of the modern movement, turns back the clock and the century in order to map the future, and rejects the indulgences of post-modernism, so too as we come full circle there will be a return to a pure photography and an understanding of the possibilities within the rectangle of the frame, even the possibilities of the black and white photograph. I think this is what Issey meant when he once said, 'Photography has become too complicated.'

Following the rise of Issey, a revolution in fashion design continued, generating a proliferation of photographic imagery that broke with the conventions of fashion photography. Photographs were used not as illustration, but as an extension of the fashion itself, as the language of the cloth was extended to the imagery of the photograph to create a cumulative and often oblique image that went beyond fashion, beyond style, and was beyond 'Japan' from its conception.

The most audacious designer to emerge in the late Seventies and early Eighties was Rei Kawakubo, a freelance fashion stylist, who then established her own company in Tokyo in 1973 under the label Comme des Garçons. The name was said to be chosen for purely euphonic reasons, but like every detail of Rei Kawakubo's work, it was precise; the connotations were neither Japanese nor feminine. By 1982 Comme des Garçons had opened in Paris; in 1986 a Comme des Garçons photography show was held at the Centre Georges Pompidou, and in 1987 Rei Kawakubo's installation at the Fashion Institute of Technology in New York, in the exhibition *Three Women: Madeleine Vionnet, Claire McCardell and Rei Kawakubo*, was regarded as a triumph by the *New York Times** in the same piece that reviewed Gerhard Richter's latest paintings. Such was the directness and force of Kawakubo's presentation that Comme des Garçons became a source, not just the name of a clothing design. She was operating within the industry with great skill and selling her product, yet winning serious respect and criticism from a wider arena. She represented a remarkable balance between commerce and creativity. New Yorkers could go to her store in SoHo as they could to Mary Boone's gallery on West Broadway. De Kooning, Schnabel, Clemente, and Leo Castelli all modelled her clothes. Her cast was unconventional; her male models were not necessarily young, but they were enigmatic or rarefied by the process. Rei Kawakubo established the authority of an artist, and she remained elusive and shy, concentrating intensely on her work away from the public glare.

Beyond the fashion, which was highly innovative and the primary focus, there were three elements which contributed to the presence of her organisation. Firstly, her

*Roberta Smith, *New York Times*, 13 March 1987.

Following spread Comme des Garçons, from *Six*, Number 6, Tokyo, 1990. Photograph – Brian Griffin; model – John Cale.

fashion shows were staged as theatre in unusual surroundings, in which the clothes were set against a space, which by association became a Kawakubo environment. Secondly, her shops were architectural extensions of her 'look'. They suggested simplicity and space. They were discreet to the point of avoiding all the formulae of window dressing. In the first shops she used raw concrete and unfinished plaster, and concrete roof tiles were used for the floor of her installation at the Fashion Institute of Technology. Ando himself, in a published conversation with Rei Kawakubo, referred to the wonderful qualities and variety of surfaces obtainable with concrete.* Though colour has now entered her range, its presence was heightened since her whole 'look' is monochromatic. Her revolution was to return to a point of minimal concentration, employing the art of reduction to point zero, then expanding from there. She also designs the furniture within her spaces. The third element is the design of her catalogues and magazines, and the use of the photograph on the page.

In 1988 Rei Kawakubo launched a Comme des Garçons magazine called *Six*. It has a large format and a print-run which has now reached 26,000, which is large for a publication of such quality. It is not for sale, but is given away to the appropriate readership. In the first issue, following photographs by André Kertész and of Cocteau, and furniture design by Eileen Gray from the Twenties, there was a statement from Kawakubo's fellow fashion designer, Yohji Yamamoto:

> If one's sense of fashion is called 'intellectual', it is already out of date and lacks originality. It may have been valid seven or eight years ago . . . Fashion has already broken through the barrier created by the accepted standard of beauty, the stated sense of what is beautiful, and will increasingly disregard conventional notions of what it should be . . . I feel a purely intuitive approach to fashion design will be increasingly important.†

The title of *Six* correspondingly referred to a sixth sense. Yamamoto's statement was a signal that Rei Kawakubo was going to follow her instincts in any direction and *Six* was the platform through which her fashion would be presented. After the first issue all text virtually disappeared; in the next four there were collaborations with Gilbert and George and Enzo Cucchi, and the use of extended sequences of photographs by Josef Koudelka, Saul Leiter and Robert Frank.

The sixth issue of *Six* took on an iconic, almost religious tone, opening with pages of the work of the Georgian primitive painter, Niko Pirosmani. English photographer, Brian Griffin, photographed models on the Georgian plains, amidst the Georgians, as if they had walked off the steppes. Rei Kawakubo had found her place. After crosses against the horizon, the sequence took one to a candlelit interior. John Cale, of *Velvet Underground* fame, was shot by Griffin as if in the depths of an Orthodox church. Rei Kawakubo had created her own landscape in Georgia as she had in the dirt of the sidewalks of New York,

*Tadao Ando and Rei Kawakubo, 'Aesthetics of Monochrome', *Hi-Pop Design Series*, Tokyo, 1985.

†Yohji Yamamoto, Comme des Garçons, *Six*, no.1, Tokyo, 1988.

Previous pages Comme des Garçons, from *Six*, Number 6, Tokyo, 1990. Photograph – Brian Griffin; model – John Cale.

through Saul Leiter's photographs. These landscapes were then inhabited by her fashion, just as her interiors harboured her clothes. She filled the entire screen of one's perception.

Comme des Garçons suffered the obvious categorisation of 'Japanese' design when it reached the West in the Eighties. 'I'm not very happy to be classified as another Japanese designer,' Rei Kawakubo declared. 'There is no one characteristic that all Japanese designers have. Each is an individual, with individual tastes.'* She wanted to dissociate herself from a sense of collective culture and from fashion history itself. Her starting point was always her stated zero.

From my first meeting with Rei Kawakubo several years ago in Tokyo, I was impressed by the visual relief of the working environment of Comme des Garçons in Aoyama, as well as by the grace and formality of her assistants. The ritualised formality of the meetings was a sign of the efficiency of the machinery. At our last meeting, despite previous discussions, I could not refrain from asking an almost taboo question: 'Rei, are you a *Japanese* designer?'

Her assistants recoiled at the question, understandably, as if I had committed an appalling social misdemeanour. However I wanted to know where the axis of her creativity resided. She is free to travel the world as much as her schedule allows. Her own landscape can be claimed anywhere from Georgia to Ulan Bator. She replied that she was no longer aware of Japan in the way I meant. After she travelled she simply came home, and that was the place where she worked. I then realised that Japan was not a question for her, since she had no need to analyse an East/West dialogue. She had travelled past that long ago. She inhabited rectangular, white rooms with monochrome tones and calm, focused spaces, and she inhabited the world.

Beyond the window there was the sound of drilling and I opened the white blinds. The skyline was filled with cranes and the skeletons of buildings. A huge hole was being bored a few feet away. It was a scene of confusion, from which the new Aoyama evolves each day in this transitory city.

'Is your design, your order, your space, a response to this chaos?' I asked her.

'What chaos?' she replied. 'What is chaos?'

The meeting was uncomfortable for it forced me to doubt the simplest ideas of order and chaos. At the moment you think you understand Japan, it shifts or the fantasy changes. Just as I destroy one fiction I call Japan, Rei Kawakubo deals another one she thinks is Georgia. Japan is the place where the questions are posed.

Eiko Ishioka, the art director and set designer, is dedicated to destroying the clichés of Japan, and since she now works in theatre and cinema, she understands the language of fantasy: 'Fantasy is necessary for human beings. Without fantasy we cannot relate to anybody and relationships are difficult. We need the veil of fantasy because the truth is too hard. But fantasy can make us blind. Today communication is instant through technology. We can reach the moon, but misunderstanding is huge.' She was referring to David Hwang's play *M. Butterfly*, which she had designed for productions in New York (1988) and London (1989). 'The events in the play happened in reality at the end of the twentieth century. The

Women's Wear Daily, New York, 1 March 1983.

179

Above and opposite Eiko Ishioka: scenery and costume design for *M. Butterfly* by David Henry Hwang, produced by Stuart
Ostrow, directed by John Dexter with lighting by Andy Phillips, 1988. Photograph – Kunihiro Shinohara.

Following spreads Eiko Ishioka: production design for *Mishima* — a film directed by Paul Schrader,
produced by Francis Ford Coppola and George Lucas, with cinematography by John Bailey and music by Philip Glass, 1985.
Photographs — Masayoshi Sukita, Katsuaki Furudate.

play raises many questions, it does not necessarily provide answers.'

The fantasy of the Orient, the *Madame Butterfly* myth, was the target of Hwang's play. He based it on the true story of a French diplomat's liaison with a Beijing opera singer, his 'Butterfly', who committed a double deception since she was both a Chinese spy and, in reality, a man. Eiko designed the play so that the theatre contained the clichés of Orientalism, then destroyed them. The sets were a cross between Oriental simplicity and Soviet constructivist theatre. Under a sweeping red arch, a square, black platform occupied the centre stage. Red lattice screens would slide open and close to define an inner space. An arc of a ramp curved round the stage and offered a descent from above as if to suggest a *hanamichi*, an extension of the *kabuki* stage that serves as a walkway out into the audience. The geometrical abstraction of the stage was balanced between curves and rectilinear forms, between red and black.

In the play's opening scene, in a prison cell in Paris in 1988, the 'Butterfly' descended the ramp in Chinese silks to the sound of the Beijing opera which faded into Puccini, as a gorgeous silk banner of a butterfly on a yellow background was unfurled from above. By proclamations of time and place, the play shifted through history and geography: Nagasaki 1904, Beijing 1960, Paris 1968–70, Hunan 1970, and back to Paris 1988. The play encompassed Pinkerton, the Indo-China War, the Vietnam War, the student revolts of the Sixties, and the Cultural Revolution. It covered a history of diametrical opposites through a century of cultural confrontation. It suggested a world split by colonialism, chauvinism, and ignorance, and a world fuelled by sex in which Asia was a submissive female while the rampant West blundered to impotence and defeat. 'There is a vision of the Orient that I have', says the diplomat, 'of slender women in *chong sams* and *kimonos* who die for the love of unworthy, foreign devils.'

The play was, of course, David Hwang's fantasy. He had never been to Beijing. Brought up in the West, he is an Asian outside Asia. His imaginary Beijing is a place like the prison cell in the play, where the artist can become Butterfly through the imagination. For Eiko Ishioka, the play was the perfect vehicle through which her creativity could reach audiences in the West, and through which she could transcend the Japanese label, just as she could transcend the label of art director or set designer. She is a multiple creative force, who has moved beyond design and beyond Japan to become an artist on her own territory.

After beginning in the Sixties as a graphic designer for a cosmetics company, Eiko became a great graphic designer in a society bent on packaging its virulent consumerism. As art director for CBS/Sony her graphic ingenuity was married to an institution at the centre of the technological revolution. She was also re-presenting to the Japanese market-place the cultural icons of the West from Leonard Bernstein to Miles Davis. In the Seventies she collaborated with Issey Miyake in staging his fashions shows, so moving without inhibition from the two dimensions of a graphic surface to a three-dimensional theatrical space. Under the auspices of Parco, the youth subsidiary of the department giant, Seibu, she created an exuberant visual image incorporated into a global ideology. She attacked Japanese insularity with imagery drawn from Africa or Rajasthan. An exotic human spectrum suggested that Parco was a world of liberated exploration for a closeted and conformist generation. Parco challenged passive consumerism. The dynamic of Eiko's

Opposite Eiko Ishioka, Shiro Kuramata, Issey Miyake: designs for *L'Inhumaine*, produced by Patrick Brunie, with music by Jean-Christophe Desnoux, Tokyo, 1990. Photograph – Hiroshi Oshima, Fusako Kodama.

imagery suggested action and participation in the world, not idle consumption. In addition to the posters the medium for the age was the television commercial. Eiko was disciplined by the condensing of the impact into the valuable seconds of the message. Her success within that field was a reflection of the power of her antennae, her sensitivity to a wide world. Her signal was in perfect synchronism with the time.

Eiko's multiplicity always presented her with problems of identity. When she first left Japan in the mid-Sixties, clutching a portfolio of designs for advertising, film, and theatre, she was told by prominent New York designers to specialise. When she reached Europe she found a design world dominated by men. To be assertive and true to the breadth of her ability, she had to return to Japan. By the mid-Seventies she was ready to close her Tokyo studio. The cultural metropolis of New York was her destination, but even there the depth of Western ignorance of modern Japan shocked her. The old images of *samurai*, *sumo*, *kabuki* and *Noh* were the residual emblems of Japan. Eiko was angered by Japan's obsession with the West, and with the West's disregard for contemporary Japan.

Through the enlightened offices of Rand Castille at the Japan Society in New York, she was invited to lecture to an invited audience. The subject of her lecture was design as a mirror of culture. She wanted to address the future with an open mind. 'If we care only about tradition, we cannot survive in the future,' she stated. She prepared the lecture in 1982 and designed her invitation card stating that the whole world was her studio. The triumph of her lecture, attended even by Noguchi, resulted in the publication of her book *Eiko by Eiko* in New York and Tokyo in 1983. It was an unprecedented moment of radical publishing.

Eiko by Eiko bore no resemblance to any previous publication. It was the first book of a post-Gutenberg age in which the primacy of the printed word was displaced by the primacy of the image. It was paced as fast as video and drew the eye to a halt like a freeze-frame action. It gathered in one volume all the different elements of Eiko's design work: graphics, textiles, fashion shows, video and television commercials. In places it even reproduced the grain of the television screen, then opened its gatefold pages wide like the grand scale of Cinemascope. The jacket depicted Faye Dunaway in the role of Kannon, the Goddess of Mercy, with attendant Oriental Bodhisattvas, suggesting an extraordinary, hybrid culture. The motifs were universal with imagery from Africa, India, and the South Pacific. The world it reflected was complex and layered, spanning two decades of media revolution. To Western eyes the book was incomprehensibly seductive. It provided a glimpse of what was possible in the future.

One of Eiko's greatest sources of inspiration was Africa. She had seen Leni Riefenstahl's photographs of the Nuba of the Sudan and in the late Seventies, they seemed to break through a black and white cliché of a suffering Africa. The majestic, physical beauty of Riefenstahl's work was highly criticised in certain quarters.* Eiko installed the exhibition of the Nuba in Tokyo in 1980 and prepared a large poster campaign, which was potentially deeply shocking to the Japanese public with their taboos on nudity. The appearance of the posters on the trains and subways was an act of pure theatre.

---

*Susan Sontag, 'Fascinating Fascism', *New York Review of Books*, 6 February 1975.

Commentators found in Eiko's respect for Riefenstahl some supposed trace of Eiko's own ambition, as if Riefenstahl was her role model. It was a suggestion that infuriated her, 'Leni is one of the most talented women of the twentieth century. Unfortunately she used her talent in a very depressing way. All artists have very dangerous possibilities, especially if we need powerful patronage. She thought Hitler understood her talent, but she didn't realize that he was the most dangerous man in human history. Design is a dangerous and political subject.'

Eiko's next controversial and dangerous project was Paul Schrader's film, *Mishima* (1985), which she designed. Many leading Japanese film directors had unsuccessfully sought permission to make a film of the writer's life. Francis Ford Coppola obtained permission to produce the film with Schrader directing, but from the outset there were misgivings in Tokyo that Westerners were at work on a subject so volatile in the Japanese psyche. Eiko deplored many of Mishima's gestures, especially those directed to secure the attention of the Western press, since she believed he sustained an anachronistic notion of Japan. Eiko confessed to Schrader that she had never met Mishima, and had no admiration for him, which pleased Schrader since he wanted to make his own *Mishima*, not Eiko's.

The film, based on five sections from separate novels or writings, each with its own colour code, was combined with Mishima's final day prior to his suicide, through which the art of his writing was merged with the art of his life. The design was a triumph and gave coherence to its ambitious structure. The cast included Tadanori Yokoo. Eiko consciously staged the film with the suggestion of *kakiwari*, the backdrop for Japanese theatre. Swordsmen met in *kendo* halls in symmetrical combat against the *hinomaru* — the red circle of the Japanese flag — in graphic harmony. The Golden Pavilion opened to its centre as if hinged on a great stage, as a model for an obsessed imagination. When the drama of assassination reached a climax in *Runaway Horses*, the last section of the film, Isao, the assassin, ran over scarlet rocks and through a forest of blue trees.

Mishima has never been released in Japan. After seeing the film in New York, the poet Mutsuro Takahashi, a close friend of Mishima, called Eiko and asked how she knew him so well. He commented on the *kakiwari* style of the film: the flattened effect of *kakiwari* was a device for projecting Mishima's two-dimensional gestural language against which his complexity, sensuality and contradictions could be defined. Eiko's work is a revelation in the psychology of design.

Her stage work, recorded photographically, continued with a production of *Planet 8*, an opera by Philip Glass based on the novel by Doris Lessing. Eiko looked for projects that freed her from Oriental connotation, and in 1989 she designed the costumes for a production of Jean Genet's *The Screens*, which was full of North African association. She recently finished work on the production in Hollywood of *Closet Land* (1990), a film about political torture by Radha Bharadwaj.

A most unusual collaboration occurred with a new showing in Tokyo of Marcel L'Herbier's film *L'Inhumaine* (1923) in 1990, with designs and costumes produced by Eiko Ishioka, Issey Miyake and Shiro Kuramata. The original film included a laboratory designed by Fernand Léger where human emotions could be conquered and the dead brought back to life. The film was a masterpiece of modern design but it was only shown for four days in Paris in 1923, then vanished until its discovery in an archive in Stockholm in the mid-Eighties. It was reshown in Paris in 1986 with a new score composed by Jean-Christophe Desnoux, who collaborated with the inventor Patrick Brunie to create two new instruments – a complex synthesizer called a 'percuphone' and a huge triangular metallic plate, which also acted as a synthesizer. In Tokyo, Eiko draped the theatre, where the film was shown, in white. Issey's costumes were geometrical and at one point a singer emerged from a yellow, triangular, sculptural form, which parted like a flower leaving the singer standing like Venus on a shell. The Tokyo performance was an historical occasion in which the elements were combined in a new medium that was beyond cinema, beyond theatre, and beyond design, with new music performed on instruments that had only just been invented. It was a great futurist collaboration.

The historical cycle becomes more emphatic as the calendar marks not just the end of the century, but a new millennium. Technological and economic advance, to which Japan has made such a great contribution, can no longer be observed in an isolated, linear pattern of progress. The cycle is defined. In 1985 Ed Ruscha painted *Japan is America*; by the year 2005 cynics might suggest he could paint *America is Japan*. The travels of figures like Issey Mikaye or Eiko Ishioka to Africa, of Tadanori Yokoo to India, or of Rei Kawakubo to Georgia, suggest the desire for the discovery of archetypes, of archaic, universal imagery. The qualities of originality and authenticity will have a high premium. In a world of bonds not barriers, the artist looking for the authentic source, or for a profound sense of place, scanning history and geography, will not be excluded from the advances of technology.

In 1981 video artist Bill Viola was invited for several months to the developmental engineering department of the Sony Corporation at Atsugi, near Tokyo. Here he was able to discuss directly the technical advances of the medium. His work in Japan culminated in *Hatsu Yume* (*First Dream*, 1981). The title refers to the Japanese traditional celebration of the first day of the year. Nearly an hour long, the video takes the form of a dream which Viola equates with the camera perspective, through which the original 'camera angle' acts as a 'mind's eye'. 'It is the point of view that goes wandering at night, that can fly above mountains and walk through walls, returning safely by morning,'[*] he wrote. The significance of *Hatsu Yume* is in its imaginative optimism.

The substances of the video are light and water, the latter representing darkness. It contains a range of creative symbols, which move from darkness to light, from stillness to motion, from silence to sound, from simplicity to complexity, and from the natural world to civilisation. The sequences pass from the ocean to forests, to pilgrimages, to the dark underwater world of fish, and through the electric light of the nocturnal city, the blazing Tokyo. It is elemental and deals with the substance of Japan, the camera and the raw material of the image itself. Tokyo is the axis, which has drawn Viola, but the subject is much wider than Japan:

I was thinking about light and its relation to water and to life, and also its opposite

[*]*Bill Viola*, The Museum of Modern Art, New York, 1987.

– darkness or the night and death. I thought about how we have built entire cities of artificial light as refuge from the dark.

Video treats light like water – it becomes a fluid on the video tube. Water supports the fish like light supports the man. Land is the death of the fish. Darkness is the death of man.*

Elemental imagery became more conspicuous once I understood Viola's achievement. I found fragments that answered the ruptured world of 1945, that Kawada had photographed when he defined his map in *Chizu* (1965). I heard that on the island of Kashima (Spirit Island) in Wakayama prefecture, the biologist, Kumagusu, had found his marine specimens in the late nineteenth century. Tamotsu Fujii, photographed the island at night and had been granted access to Kumagusu's archives, where he photographed the specimens. This evidence formed a poetic exploration of the ocean and life in the whorl of seashells and the delicacy of the jawbone of a shark.

Hiroshi Sugimoto, who once photographed the empty screens and interiors of movie theatres, had photographed the oceans. The Atlantic, the Pacific, the Sea of Japan and the Caribbean compounded the sense of universality. The marine evidence of the planet was reduced to rectangles, bisected into two tones of grey, air and water.

Transcended by these photographs, Japan still acts as a source, as an intersection of past and future. As early as the fourth or fifth year of the Meiji era, photographs of the Emperor were made as albumen prints. Duplicates were spread throughout the land to reinforce his power. By the fifteenth year of Meiji, factory-made photographic paper was available and the duplicates lost some of their mystery. The Emperor no longer had to travel his land and could remain in his palace, but his power was still dependent on sunlight. During the Taisho era paper technology changed again and new pictures were made. Nightguards were posted at schools in possession of the images; people even died trying to save the photographs from fire. Carbon and gelatin technology was introduced with the Showa era and photographs of the Emperor were displayed in every elementary school. They were housed in shrines, which were only opened on special occasions by the principal wearing white gloves. The closed shrine, concealing the image, is the exterior façade, like nocturnal Tokyo, or the Imperial Palace, or the Sony Building with its walls of thousands of television screens, behind which lies another world, where the imaginary axis resides.

During the last weeks of the Emperor Hirohito, Kawada photographed the sun every day, including that of the Emperor's death, the final day of the Showa era. He has been photographing the moon and its orbit, and the eclipse of Venus and finds some unity in this series, which he calls *The Last Cosmology*. The motifs become mirror images of the Japanese flag, which he once photographed crumpled like his map. They form, simply, circles of light within rectangles of darkness.

Bill Viola, The Museum of Modern Art, New York, 1987.

Following spread Bill Viola: still from video, *Hatsu Yume (First Dream)*, 1981

Tamotsu Fujii: *Jawbone of a Shark, Specimen from Collection of Kumagusu Minakata*, 1990

Tamotsu Fujii: *Kashima Island, Site of Kumagusu Minakata's Research*, 1989

Hiroshi Sugimoto: *Caribbean Sea, Jamaica*, 1980

Hiroshi Sugimoto: *Pacific Ocean, Oregon II*, 1988

Kikuji Kawada: *The Last Sun of the Showa Era*, 7 January Showa 64, 1989

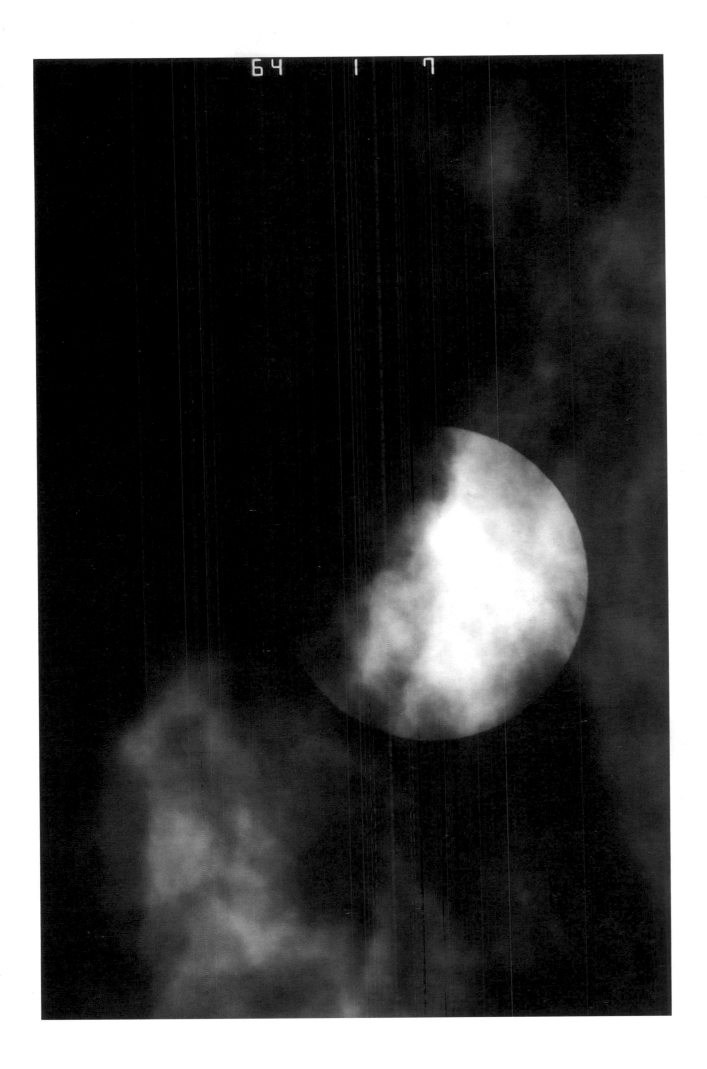

Kikuji Kawada: *The Last Sun of the Showa Era*, 7 January Showa 64, 1989

BIOGRAPHICAL

NOTES

David Byrne was born in Scotland in 1952 and moved to Baltimore when he was a child. He studied at the Rhode Island School of Design. As lead singer, guitarist and songwriter for Talking Heads he has produced a number of albums and music videos. He has collaborated with choreographer Twyla Tharp and playwright Robert Wilson. He conceived and directed his own film *True Stories* in 1986. Tokyo has been a recent subject for his photographic exploration and his photographs were published by *Parkett* in Zurich in 1990.

Comme des Garçons was established in Tokyo in 1973 by the fashion designer Rei Kawakubo who graduated from the Fine Arts, Aesthetics Department of Keio University, Tokyo in 1964. In 1981 Comme des Garçons made its début at the Paris fashion shows and Kawakubo set up an office in Paris a year later. In 1986 a Comme des Garçons photography show was held at the Centre Georges Pompidou, Paris. The following year Kawakubo's designs were shown in the exhibition *Three Women: Madeleine Vionnet, Claire McCardell and Rei Kawakubo* at the Fashion Institute of Technology, New York. In 1988 Kawakubo launched the Comme des Garçons magazine, *Six*.

Tamotsu Fujii was born in 1949. He graduated from the Tokyo Sogo Photography School and then joined the photography department of the Osaka Advertising Research Institute. He has been a freelance photographer since 1976 and has received many awards for his commercial work.

Masahisa Fukase was born on Hokkaido in 1934. He published his first book, *Homo Ludence*, in 1971. His work was included in the exhibition *New Japanese Photography* at the Museum of Modern Art, New York in 1974. His great narrative series *Ravens* was published in Tokyo in 1986, and photographs from the series were included in the exhibition *Black Sun* in Oxford and London in 1986, and the Philadelphia Museum of Art as well as other American museums.

Hiroshi Hamaya was born in Tokyo in 1915. He became a freelance photographer in 1937 and began his association with Magnum Photos in 1960. His publications include *Snow Land* (1956), *Japan's Back Coast* (1957), *America, America* (1971), and *Mount Fuji* (1978).

Tatsumi Hijikata was born in the Aomori district of northern Honshu in 1928. He was regarded as the founder of the form of dance theatre known as *Ankoku Butoh*. Hijikata arrived in Tokyo in the Fifties and absorbed flamenco, modern American dance and elements of *Die Neue Tanz* from Germany. His own dance had its roots in his childhood and his culture. He was a close friend of the writer Yukio Mishima. His greatest performance may have been *Tatsumi Hijikata and the Japanese, Revolt of the Flesh*, in 1968. He died in Tokyo in 1986.

Eikoh Hosoe was born in 1933 and established his reputation as a leading Japanese photographer after the publication of his first book, *Man and Woman*, in 1961. Since then, his work has been exhibited in museums worldwide. His other books include *Barakei*, 1963 (portraits of the writer Yukio Mishima), *Kamaitachi*, 1968 (a collaboration with the dancer Tatsumi Hijikata), *Embrace* (1971), and a study of the Spanish architect Gaudi in 1984. Hosoe is a professor at the Tokyo Institute of Polytechnics.

Eiko Ishioka received international attention as an art director and designer following the publication in New York and Tokyo of her book *Eiko by Eiko* in 1983, subsequently published in London in 1990. She has been art director for the Parco group in Tokyo and for CBS/Sony. In the Eighties she concentrated on film and stage design: she designed Paul Schrader's film *Mishima* (1985), and David Hwang's play *M. Butterfly* which opened in London in 1989. She has collaborated with Philip Glass on an opera, and designed the costumes for a production of Jean Genet's *The Screens*. Her work with the architect Arata Isozaki was shown at the *Tokyo: Form and Spirit* exhibition in Minneapolis in 1986.

Kikuji Kawada was born in Ibaragi in 1933. He graduated from the Economics Department of Rikkio University in 1956 and became a freelance photographer in 1959. His first book, *Chizu*, was published in 1965. In the Sixties he travelled extensively in Europe, America and South-east Asia. In the Seventies he worked on a long series entitled *Los Caprichos* and in 1974 his work was included in the exhibition *New Japanese Photography* at the Museum of Modern Art, New York. At the end of the Eighties he pursued his interest in astronomy and photographing the planets in a series called *The Last Cosmology*.

William Klein was born in New York in 1928. After World War II he studied painting in Paris. His first book, *New York*, was published in 1956 and was one of the most radical photography books of all time. In 1957 and '58 he made fashion photographs for *Vogue*, produced his first film, *Broadway by Light*, and published his second book, *Rome*. In 1964 his books *Moscow* and *Tokyo* were published, completing a cycle of four cities. Since the Sixties he has worked as a film-maker while continuing to photograph.

Seiji Kurata was born in Tokyo in 1945. After he graduated in 1976 from the Photographic Workshop School in Japan his work was exhibited and published in Europe. His book *Flash Up* was published in Tokyo in 1980. In the Eighties he photographed in colour throughout South-east Asia.

Issey Miyake was born in Hiroshima in 1938. He graduated from Tama Art University, Tokyo in 1964 after which he studied and worked in Paris and New York. He returned to Japan and in 1970 established the Miyake Design Studio, which became the leading fashion studio of the Seventies. His first book, *East Meets West*, was published in 1978. His exhibition *Bodyworks: Fashion Without*

Taboos was held at the Victoria and Albert Museum, London, in 1978, and his exhibition *A Ūn* was held at the Musée des Arts Décoratifs in Paris in 1988. He has been engaged in a number of collaborations with the photographer Irving Penn.

Ryuji Miyamoto was born in Tokyo in 1947 and graduated from Tama Art University, Tokyo, in 1973. He moved to Vancouver, Canada, in 1976 and travelled throughout South-east Asia and China in 1980. Since 1983 he has been photographing demolition sites in Japan and Berlin. His book *Architectural Apocalypse* was published in 1988 with an essay by the architect Arata Isozaki.

Daido Moriyama was born in 1938. He worked as a graphic designer in Osaka then moved to Tokyo and became an assistant to Eikoh Hosoe. His work has been included in all the international exhibitions of Japanese photography and his original style has greatly affected its course. He has published many books in Japan and his first book of essays, *Dog Memories*, was published in Tokyo in 1984. At the end of the Eighties he photographed in Paris and North Africa.

Masatoshi Naitoh was born in Tokyo in 1938. He graduated in Applied Science from Waseda University in 1961. He is an anthropologist with particular interest in the roots of Japanese culture. In 1966 he exhibited his photographs of mummies in Japan. After travelling for several months with a group of wandering actors and performers he exhibited his photographs of the troupe in 1970. He participated in the exhibition of New Japanese Photography at the Museum of Modern Art, New York, in 1974. His book *Tokyo* was published in 1985.

Irving Penn is one of the most distinguished portrait and fashion photographers of the post-war period. A retrospective of his work was held at the Museum of Modern Art, New York, in 1984. In 1987 he began to photograph the fashion designs of Issey Miyake and the work was published in a book *Issey Miyake: Photographs by Irving Penn* in 1988. In 1989 he produced a catalogue for Issey Miyake and in 1990 he photographed the pleats designed by Issey Miyake for the catalogue of the exhibition *Pleats Please* at the Touko Museum of Contemporary Art, Tokyo.

Hiroshi Sugimoto was born in Tokyo in 1948. He studied in both Tokyo and Los Angeles and moved to New York in 1974. In 1980 he was awarded a Guggenheim Fellowship. His work is in the collections of both the Museum of Modern Art and the Metropolitan Museum, New York, as well as other major museums throughout America.

Shuji Terayama, poet, playwright, theatre director and film-maker was born in 1935. At Waseda University he made a study of *Kabuki* theatre. His first book of poems, *To Me, the Month of May*, was published in 1957. He formed an experimental group with the dancer Tatsumi Hijikata in 1960. He was one of the founders of *Tenjosajiki*, a Laboratory of Theatre Play in 1967, and directed the group throughout Europe in the early Seventies as well as directing a number of films including *Throw Away Your Books, Let's Go Into the Streets* in 1971. His photographs were exhibited throughout Europe in the late Seventies. Terayama died in 1983.

Bill Viola was born in New York in 1951 and graduated from Syracuse University in 1973. Three years later he travelled to the Solomon Islands, South Pacific to study traditional music and dance. In 1977 he travelled to Java to record traditional performing arts. In 1979 he went to the Sahara desert to videotape mirages. In 1980 and 1981 he lived in Japan where he studied traditional culture and video technology as artist-in-residence at the laboratories of the Sony Corporation. In the Eighties he travelled to the Himalayas to study Tibetan Buddhist rituals and to Fiji to document firewalking. He received a Guggenheim Fellowship in 1985 for his work in video and an exhibition of his work was held at the Museum of Modern Art, New York, in 1987.

Tadanori Yokoo was born in Nishiwaki, Hyogo Prefecture, in 1936. In 1972 he won the UNESCO Prize for his prints and an exhibition of his work was held at the Museum of Modern Art, New York. He was the leading print and poster designer in Japan in the Sixties and Seventies. He co-founded *Tenjosajiki* with Shuji Terayama in 1967. In 1981 he became a painter and in 1984 designed ballet sets for La Scala, Milan. In 1986 he produced a series of monumental ceramic panels depicting the history of Tokyo for the *Tokyo: Form and Spirit* exhibition in Minneapolis.

ACKNOWLEDGMENTS

I WOULD LIKE to thank John Hoole of Barbican Art Gallery for initiating this project and David Godwin of Jonathan Cape for his commitment to publish the book and for all his editorial advice. I am very grateful to Carol Brown and Tomoko Sato at the Barbican for their enormous support and to Anne Newman at Cape for her clarity and precision with the manuscript.

My debts in Japan are great and all the artists have given their time and work most generously. I am particularly indebted to Jan Kawata and Yuki Maekawa of Comme des Garçons, Yasuko Ikeda at Eiko Design Inc., Midori Kitamura of the Miyake Design Studio, Kyoko Kujo of Jinriki-hikoki-sha, Akiko Motofuji of the Asbestos Theatre and the Tatsumi Hijikata Memorial Archives, Kenji Hosoe, Ei Yokoo, Kazue Kobata, Akiko Ohtake, Tatsuo Fukushima, and Yuriko Kuchiki. I would like to thank the family of Kikuji Kawada for all their kindness, and above all my special thanks to Kazuko, Tetsuya and Osamu Uehara for their generosity over the years.

Finally this book emerges after several years of discussion and prompting with my friends in New York, Nicholas Callaway, Dorothy Norman and Ingrid Sischy, to whom I extend my thanks.

M H

Beyond Japan: A Photo Theatre
First published 1991
© Mark Holborn 1991
Barbican Art Gallery, Barbican Centre, London EC2Y 8DS
in association with
Jonathan Cape, 20 Vauxhall Bridge Road, London SW1V 2SA

Barbican Art Gallery gratefully acknowledges the generous support of
QUICK EUROPE LIMITED.

QUICK
QUICK EUROPE LIMITED

For fast, reliable
market information

Mark Holborn has asserted his right
under the Copyright, Designs and Patents Act, 1988
to be identified as the author of this work

ISBN 0–946372–23–3

Designed by Lynn Boulton and Mark Holborn

Cover photograph by Kikuji Kawada: *The Last Eclipse of the Sun,*
11.23 a.m., 18 March 1988, Ogasawara, Tokyo, from *The Last Cosmology*

Typeset by Falcon Graphic Art Ltd
Colour separations by Leeds Photolitho Ltd, Leeds, Yorkshire
Printed in Italy by Amilcare Pizzi, Milan